For Vera N __
thanks for your __
and encouragement!
Marvin   'Columbia, MO
              5/31/91

ETHNICITY and IDENTITY in CONTEMPORARY AFRO-VENEZUELAN LITERATURE

ETHNICITY and IDENTITY in CONTEMPORARY AFRO-VENEZUELAN LITERATURE

A Culturalist Approach

MARVIN A. LEWIS

University of Missouri Press
Columbia and London

Library of Congress Cataloging-in-Publication Data

Lewis, Marvin A.
    Ethnicity and identity in contemporary Afro-Venezuelan literature:
    a culturalist approach / Marvin A. Lewis
        p.   cm.
    Includes bibliographical references and index.
    ISBN 0-8262-0840-1 (alk. paper)
        1. Venezuelan literature—Black authors—History and criticism.
    2. Venezuelan literature—20th century—History and criticism.
    3. Blacks in literature.   4. Race awareness in literature.
    I. Title.
    PQ8538.L46   1992   92-4224
    860.9'896087—dc20   CIP

∞™ This paper meets the requirements of the
American National Standard for Permanence of Paper
for Printed Library Materials, Z39.48, 1984.

Designer: Kristie Lee
Typesetter: Connell-Zeko Type & Graphics
Printer and Binder: Thomson-Shore, Inc.
Typefaces: Palatino, Kabel Medium and Bold

For Judy, Monica, and Kevin—Latin Lovers

CONTENTS

ACKNOWLEDGMENTS

Thanks to the Research Council of the University of Missouri-Columbia for granting me money and a leave of absence from 1989 to 1990, and to the NEH Travel to Collections Program for support of research travel to Caracas. Thanks also to Dr. James Scott in Venezuela for his assistance and the use of his library; to Vera Mitchell, University of Illinois-Urbana, for sending me books; to Jamaine Shipley, Judi Dawson, and Mary Harris for manuscript preparation and editorial assistance.

All translations from Spanish into English are my own.

ETHNICITY and IDENTITY in CONTEMPORARY AFRO-VENEZUELAN LITERATURE

INTRODUCTION

Afro-Venezuelan Literature: A Culturalist Approach

The real problem for the critic is not so much to be in tune
with the critical times, as to tune in to the specific music of a
voice, the specific tonalities of a work.

—Victor Brombert

This book is an analysis of four important works, published between 1938 and 1977, that offer interpretations of the black experience in Venezuela. The authors and texts are: Juan Pablo Sojo
(1907–1948), *Nochebuena negra* (*Black St. John's Eve*, 1943); Ramón
Díaz Sánchez (1903–1968), *Cumboto* (1950); Manuel Rodríguez Cárdenas (1912–1991), *Tambor: Poemas para negros y mulatos* (*Drum: Poems
for Blacks and Mulattoes*, 1938); and Antonio Acosta Márquez (1944–),
Yo pienso aquí donde . . . Estoy (*I Think Right Here Where . . . I Am*,
1977, 1981). Additional relevant writings by these authors are discussed in an effort to illuminate different aspects of the writers and
their works. While a number of articles and book chapters have
been devoted to the novels of Sojo and Díaz Sánchez, their contributions have not been discussed alongside those of Rodríguez Cárdenas and Acosta Márquez as comparative components of the larger
Afro-Venezuelan dilemma.

By examining this body of literature, it is possible to see a process
of deafricanization and a movement toward miscegenation occurring thematically, linguistically, and mythically. Recently, however,
there has been an attempt by Venezuelan writers to reemphasize
the importance of the African heritage in Venezuelan literature.
These two opposing trends are illustrative of the ambiguous attitudes toward color and ethnicity in Venezuelan letters. At the center
of this study are the concepts of minority discourse and Afrocentricity, both of which are concerned with establishing a worldview
about the writing and speaking of oppressed black people.

My critical approach is culturalist; by using the term *culturalist* I
mean that my evaluation is based on the notion that Afro-Venezuelan literature is culturally unique because it expresses some of the
distinctive features of Afro-Venezuelan shared, learned behavior.

1

The critical model for this type of approach and its applicability to ethnic literature was outlined by the late Joseph Sommers in his evaluation of Chicano literature of the United States.[1] The central concern of culturalist criticism in Venezuela is to identify and analyze that country's cultural features: its notions of an African past, its myths, its linguistic and thematic survivals, its folk beliefs, its societal iniquities, and its development of an Afro-Venezuelan worldview. The culturalist method combines elements of both formalist and historical/dialectical criticism in close readings of the texts. Each work is examined using this methodology.

Following these brief explanatory comments, the Introduction undertakes an assessment of writing treating the black presence in Venezuela, including two important collections of essays interpreting the Afro-Venezuelan experience: *Cam, ensayo sobre el negro* (*Ham, Essay on the Negro*, 1933) by Ramón Díaz Sánchez and *Temas y apuntes afro-venezolanos* (*Afro-Venezuelan Themes and Notes*, 1943) by Juan Pablo Sojo. These are two serious evaluations of black origins, history, customs, and other manifestations of culture. *Ham* is the first published book to analyze the impact of blacks upon Venezuelan national culture, while *Afro-Venezuelan Themes and Notes* defines the African dimension of that cultural entity.

Chapter 1 of this study, "*Nochebuena negra:* The Essence of the Darker Brother/Sister," analyzes Juan Pablo Sojo's landmark novel. Myth, folklore, customs, and other cultural aspects are posited by Sojo to be in constant play between fiction and fact, fantasy and reality. This work is the most important fictional affirmation of black culture published to date in Venezuela. It is analyzed here as fiction which interprets reality.

Chapter 2, "*Cumboto:* Let Us All Miscegenate," is a discussion of the most profound literary interpretation of miscegenation and identity in Venezuelan literature. *Cumboto* focuses upon ethnic lynching as a national practice designed to whiten blacks out of existence in the country; it represents the culminating point of Ramón Díaz Sánchez's attempt to develop a mulatto perspective in literature.

Chapter 3, "*Tambor:* The Black/White Dialectic," is an analysis of the first published book of poetry that interprets the Afro-Venezuelan experience. Though not well received by the literary establishment in Venezuela because of its content, *Drum* remains a classic work of Spanish-American *negrista* writing. Stylistically and thematically, the poet incorporates some of the basic characteristics of

1. "From the Critical Premise to the Product: Critical Modes and Their Applications to a Chicano Literary Text."

Afro-Venezuelan culture outlined by Díaz Sánchez and Sojo in *Ham* and *Afro-Venezuelan Themes and Notes.*[2]

Chapter 4, *"Yo pienso aquí donde . . . Estoy:* On Being and Not Being Black in Venezuela," examines Antonio Acosta Márquez's groundbreaking collection of popular poems that express serious social concerns. At the core of this poetry is a sense of estrangement, a feeling of both physical and spiritual loss. The central importance of this book is that it expresses precisely what many scholars maintain does not exist: an awareness by the people of Venezuela of their blackness. *I Think Right Here Where . . . I Am* is both an affirmation of Venezuelan *negritud* and the culmination of a poetic process of affirmation that began, ironically, with Rodríguez Cárdenas four decades earlier.

The Conclusion, "If Not Now, When?" discusses the intertextual nature of these works and others depicting the problematic existence of black literature in Venezuela. It also assesses the current status of Afro-Venezuelan literary studies vis-à-vis the broader context of Venezuelan literature, suggesting further what has to be done to assure that blacks are presented in the creative and critical literature as integral components of the national ethos.

In a recent article entitled "Minority Discourse and the African Collective: Some Examples from Latin American and Caribbean Literature," the late Josaphat B. Kubayanda makes some observations that are relevant to Afro-Venezuelan literature. He writes regarding minority discourse and the form and content of its expression:

> Minority discourse necessarily reflects cultural contacts and the problems that they generate and nurse. When some of the problems of the real world of cultural contacts are translated into imaginative writing, as they are in the multiple texts in the Black Latin American literary tradition, we as real readers are invited, as it were, to consider the protagonists or the poetic voices, themselves nearly always completely "drained of their essence," as they pose and examine crucial group questions on genealogy, identity, and existential anguish. Who are *we*? What have *we* done? What has been done to *us*? What can *we* do? Where are *we* going? These are some of the major questions an Afro-Latin minority discourse addresses.[3]

Afro-Venezuelan literature certainly examines questions of origins, presence, and future in regard to blacks in Venezuelan society. At

---

2. In a letter dated July 13, 1990, to the editors of the *Afro-Hispanic Review,* Manuel Rodríguez Cárdenas refers to *Tambor* as "mi poesía negroide" (my blackish poetry).
3. "Minority Discourse and the African Collective," 116.

the same time, this written expression has proven over the years to be an attempt to create a minority discourse. Questions of genealogy, identity, and existential anguish have been addressed from multiple perspectives, whether from the pens of well-meaning mestizo writers and vacillating mulattoes like Manuel Rodríguez Cárdenas and Ramón Díaz Sánchez, or from the pens of black writers such as Juan Pablo Sojo and Antonio Acosta Márquez. These multiple perspectives are apparent in this brief examination of some of the critical literature devoted to looking at blacks in Venezuela from a multidisciplinary perspective.

In spite of the attention given to Afro-Venezuelan culture by researchers, little serious criticism has been devoted to creative literature. Literature of the black experience in Venezuela is usually read as folkloric and quaint, but not worthy of rigorous critical scrutiny. Recent studies such as *La cultura afrovenezolana en sus escritores contemporáneos* (*Afro-Venezuelan Culture in Its Contemporary Writers*, 1982) by Daniel Piquet and *Poblaciones y culturas negras de Venezuela* (*Black Populations and Cultures of Venezuela*, 1983) by Alfredo Chacón are but two attempts, employing different methodologies, to arrive at an understanding of exactly what constitutes the Afro element in Venezuelan culture. These two studies build upon earlier research by Miguel Acosta Saignes, Juan Liscano, José Marcial Ramos Guédez, Angelina Pollak-Eltz, Pedro Lhaya, and others who have either affirmed or denied the importance of Afro-Venezuelan culture.

Piquet's *Afro-Venezuelan Culture* is a socio-literary evaluation of *Pobre negro* (*Poor Black*) by Romulo Gallegos, *Cumboto* by Ramón Díaz Sánchez, *Canción de negros* (*Song of Blacks*) by Guillermo Meneses, and *Eladia* by Julio Garmendia. *Cumboto* is the only one of these prose works written with the intention of presenting the perspectives of Afro-Venezuelans. Piquet also includes chapters on "Oral Literature" and "The Black and Rhythm." He explains that "beginning with the works and authors chosen, we shall try to point out and explain the black elements that constitute a constant in Venezuelan culture. For that we shall utilize essentially works of such quality that may permit the most complete and direct study possible of Venezuelan culture."[4] Piquet succeeds in presenting essentially an analysis of outsiders' interpretations of black culture in the works of Gallegos, Díaz Sánchez, Meneses, and Garmendia. For an evaluation of this nature, one would have expected the critic to use other seminal works, like Manuel Rodríguez Cárdenas's *Drum* and Juan Pablo Sojo's *Black St. John's Eve*, as points of departure.

4. *La cultura afrovenezolana en sus escritores contemporáneos*, 18.

Chacón's brief study takes an anthropological perspective, tracing the origins of Afro-Venezuelans, assessing their present-day communities, and commenting upon their current status. In Chapter 4, which is devoted to "The Afro-Venezuelan Components of the National Culture," Chacón points out five geographical areas where the majority of blacks are concentrated, and he discusses their cultural contributions under the headings of "Music and Poetry" and "Magical Religious Activity." His emphasis is on "popular culture."[5]

Another important study related to aspects of Afro-Venezuelan culture discussed by both Piquet and Chacón is *El folklore en la novela venezolana* (*Folklore in the Venezuelan Novel*, 1981) by Luis Felipe Ramón y Rivera. This is a systematic and thorough discussion of folkloric elements in a dozen novels, including *Cumboto* and *Black St. John's Eve*. The topics that are discussed in relation to Venezuelan society are "Sayings," "Riddles," "Empirical Knowledge," "Earthly Festive Customs," "Nonfestive Customs," and "Oral Literature." These three studies by Piquet, Chacón, and Ramón y Rivera demonstrate that "culture" and "folklore" are two elements of the black Venezuelan experience that have been examined recently, thus indicating that creative writing is indeed a key ingredient for studying that population.

It is my opinion that any serious examination of contemporary Afro-Venezuelan culture should take into account early attempts at its evaluation, such as Ramón Díaz Sánchez's *Ham* and Juan Pablo Sojo's *Afro-Venezuelan Themes and Notes*. In these two studies, one finds serious assessments of black origins, history, customs, religion, and the general relationship of blacks to Venezuelan culture. Most of the current studies of Afro-Venezuelan culture do not improve greatly upon what was written by Sojo decades ago. Therefore, these two authors will be my points of departure in this culturalist attempt to interpret some of the relationships between literature and society in Afro-Venezuelan literature.

Díaz Sánchez's *Ham* is probably the first serious attempt in book form to assess the impact of blacks upon Venezuelan national culture. *Cumboto*, his novel, is the best literary interpretation of the themes of *mestizaje* and identity that are prevalent in that country. The highly acclaimed and widely published Díaz Sánchez has contributed to all genres of Venezuelan literature, with *Cumboto* representing the culminating point in his trajectory as a novelist.

Díaz Sánchez addresses, in ambivalent fashion, the African pres-

5. *Poblaciones y culturas negras de Venezuela*, 51–69.

ence in Venezuela on several occasions. In *Ambito y acento: Para una teoría de la venezolanidad* (*Limit and Accent: Toward a Theory of Venezuelaness*, 1938) he devotes one of five chapters to the biblical metaphor of "Ham" that had been elaborated by him five years before. This metaphor, which explains why Ham's black descendants are condemned to wander, is a commonplace in the literature of many South American writers. In his chapter, Díaz Sánchez assesses the experiences of the blacks from their arrival as slaves in Venezuela in the early decades of the sixteenth century to the 1930s. His attitude toward the *negro* is basically positive as he attempts to correct misconceptions:

> Among the exaggerations that are committed with frequency at the cost of American history is that of attributing to the black element all the responsibility of the inferiority complexes of the neo-American. All that signifies backwardness, cultural stagnation, social anarchy, refers to the black, whose bloody comportment is considered the obstacle which has impeded those countries from entering in an open process of civilization.[6]

Díaz Sánchez goes on to state that these accusations and exaggerations are based upon ignorance regarding black culture, and he attempts to rectify the situation through a cogent discussion of the African experience in Spanish America. His analysis touches upon cultural features such as religion, beauty, humor, miscegenation, and the mulatto, all from a positive perspective.

Díaz Sánchez's view of the Venezuelan black projected in *Limit and Accent* is an advancement over the negative image of this group presented in the original version of *Ham*. First published in installments in the Caracas magazine *Arquero* in October 1932, *Ham* is divided into ten brief chapters in which negative stereotypes are apparent. Under the topic "Antiheroicism of the Black," the author writes, "The black is ugly. It is also said, almost generally, that he is a coward. But I will limit myself to saying that he is anti-heroic, which is not the same."[7]

Díaz Sánchez concludes that he does not view the Venezuelan black as a real "problem" but rather as a danger to the moral and spiritual fiber of the homeland. Summing up his arguments in *Ham*, Díaz Sánchez reiterates some of his concerns which have been noted earlier: "I don't believe that the moral scars which make the black

6. *Ambito y acento: Para una teoría de la venezolanidad,* 70. The segment of the chapter "Ham" devoted to the *mulato* is an expanded version of a statement published by Díaz Sánchez as a contribution to the July 3, 1938, *El Heraldo* article, "Ensayo: Averiguación del mulato en *Tambor,*" an essay on Manuel Rodríguez Cárdenas's *Drum.*
7. *Cam,* 27.

inferior to other races are an intrinsic inferiority. But yes, I have the conviction that the atavism created by a super-secular environment has condemned him to not redeem himself while his pigmentation and facial angle are not modified."[8] Therefore, in order for the black to become an integral component of society, he must undergo both mental and physical transformations. Following Díaz Sánchez's line of reasoning, this transformation will require a distancing from the African physical norm and a movement toward the miscegenated ethnic center.

Ramón Díaz Sánchez leaves no doubt that the future of Venezuela belongs to the *mulato*, whom he refers to in *Limit and Accent* as "the awakening product of the great fusion": "With the weapon of his smile and sensuality the mulatto goes, now free, climbing toward civil heights, conquering the medium he craves: the city. Because this new being is eminently urban. Tenacious as an acid, his spirit saturates everything: the street, the shop, commerce, the church, the forum, the academy, all that which formed the shield of Hispanic domination."[9] While Díaz Sánchez is enthused about the *mulato* and the social progress of this group, there are still obstacles: "The Creole and peninsular aristocracy continues exercising despotic domination of the society, and their pragmatics seem more severe because of the clash they produce with the customs of the prolific brown hierarchy."[10] Díaz Sánchez envisions the old Creole aristocracy being replaced by a *mulato* class that will dominate social institutions and continue to revitalize a stagnant European culture.

As an essayist, Díaz Sánchez remains inconsistent in his view regarding the positive contributions of Africans to Venezuelan culture. In *Paisaje histórico de la cultura venezolana* (*Historic Landscape of Venezuelan Culture*, 1965), published three years before his death, Díaz Sánchez devotes a chapter to "Indians, Hispanics, and Africans." In the section "What the African Brought," he discusses important manifestations of Afro-Venezuelan culture: "mythology, mimeticism, gift of the word, poetry, humor, detachment."[11] Díaz Sánchez concludes reluctantly that in spite of official denials, blacks have left indelible marks on all aspects of Venezuelan life: biological, spiritual, and material.

In both *Afro-Venezuelan Themes and Notes* and *Black St. John's Eve*, Juan Pablo Sojo purports to define the African dimension of Vene-

8. Ibid., 36–37.
9. *Ambito y acento*, 83.
10. Ibid., 84.
11. *Paisaje histórico de la cultura venezolana*, 30.

zuelan culture. The novel, *Black St. John's Eve*, is an interpretation of the black experience in the Barlovento region, while the essays of *Afro-Venezuelan Themes and Notes* treat, in depth, the questions of ethnicity and identity. Folklore, the oral tradition, customs, magic, dances, and other aspects of culture are well within the scope of Sojo's study. In fact, much of what is found in recent Afro-Venezuelan studies owes a great deal to this pioneer, although he is not always given credit.

Afro-Venezuelan Themes and Notes is a powerful discussion of the impact of Africans upon Venezuelan society. Sojo's premise is that the blacks in Venezuela have had less of an impact than their counterparts in Haiti and Brazil because of the process of deafricanization and the push toward miscegenation in Venezuela. His approach reflects the ambiguity of questions regarding class and race in that country.

Afro-Venezuelan Themes and Notes is divided into six sections: "Differences" compares the ethnic situation in the Antilles and Brazil with Venezuela; "Customs, Superstition, Witchcraft" contrasts African remnants throughout Latin America; "Aritualism and Magic" discusses authentic Afro-Venezuelan rituals; "The Black Presence in Venezuela" addresses the "non-existent" black problem in Venezuela; "Prejudice—Notes on a Problem" deals with skin color; and "General Facts About Witchcraft and Healing" examines the magical world of Afro-Venezuelans through case histories.

Perhaps more than an affirmer of Afro-Venezuelan culture in his essays, Sojo's perspective is that of an assimilationist who views the Afro component as not being any more unique than the indigenous or the Spanish components. How, then, does the Afro element fit into the equation?

In the second section of the book, Sojo makes a remark that will echo his argument regarding the cultural dimension of Afro-Venezuelans: "Neither Olorún, nor Obatalá, or Yemanyá signify things or idolotric representations in our environment which establish an association between the adored image and the personification of forgotten cults. There remains only the dregs, hereditary reflections in the known dances, songs, and legends which incarnate the profoundly ritualistic character of the black."[12] The theoretical underpinning for Sojo's study is *Los negros brujos* (*The Black Sorcerers*), the classic study of Afro-Cuban culture by Fernando Ortiz. What Sojo constantly brings to bear on his own study is that the black experience in Venezuela is diametrically opposed to that of Cuba;

12. *Temas y apuntes afro-venezolanos*, 14.

according to Sojo, neither the numbers of blacks nor the opportunities for cultural maintenance are as great in South America as in
the Caribbean. Therefore, it is no surprise that he writes, "In our
midst the motley figures of African fetishes so common among the
blacks of Brazil and the Antilles are unknown."[13]

Sojo is not very clear either regarding the issues of class and
ethnicity:

> We cannot speak in Venezuela of a specifically black problem. The
> problem is of a universal character and is anchored within the
> social problems which today confront the world and which some
> barbarous people wish to resolve with violence, casting aside that
> way the truth of civilization. The presence of our *Afro* manifests
> itself as we have stated in the beliefs and customs common to all
> Venezuelans more than in physiological characteristics, such as
> the deformation of the lip, gruffness, skin color, etc.[14]

These words repeat the theory set forth in the dominant Venezuelan social ideology regarding the nonproblematic nature of being
black in Venezuela. Theoretically, Venezuelans are not judged by
the color of their skin, an issue on which Sojo contradicts himself:

> Well then, in the concrete case of Venezuela, the problem has its
> peculiar aspects. Here one only has *the prejudice of skin color.* In that
> is differentiated truly our problem from that which exists in other
> nations. That results above all in a misrepresentation if we take
> into account the fact that all Venezuelans—at least the majority—
> have something of blackness. Nevertheless, the prejudice of skin
> color painfully paralyzes our national life.[15]

Sojo recognizes that there is a pigmentocracy in Venezuela, but he
hesitates to admit that color/ethnicity is the most important inhib-
itor to black progress in that country. His attitude is mainstream.

Sojo ends the discussion of Afro-Venezuelan culture with an il-
lustrated discussion of *brujería* (witchcraft) and *curanderismo* (folk
healing), focusing upon individual cases from all regions of the
country. He cautions that the world of "magic" is not the exclusive
realm of the Afro element; this is consistent with his view that
blacks are merely one of three integral components of Venezuelan
society.

The important question regarding literature explored in *Afro-Ven-*

13. Ibid., 19.
14. Ibid., 12.
15. Ibid., 33.

ezuelan Themes and Notes is whether attitudes taken by an essayist will necessarily be integrated into a work of fiction. Will ideologies be transposed from one genre to the other by the author for the sake of consistency in his worldview? Or does the reader of fiction expect the same dynamism and ambiguity found within a far-from-static culture?

Since Venezuela prides itself on being one of the most miscegenated countries in South America, there has been strong resistance to the concept of "Afro-Venezuelan" in general and "Afro-Venezuelan literature" in particular. Although mainstream Venezuelan intellectuals have studied the culture of Venezuelans of African descent for decades and written about them from a distance, attempts to produce literature with a distinctly Afrocentric voice have been met with hostility by many critics and publishers. Their attitude has been that blacks are a part of the national culture and do not have an expression that is different from the norm. Many Afro-Venezuelans seem to have bought the miscegenation argument hook, line, and sinker. Yet, they do not seem to be aware or care that this attitude, which can be summed up as "we share a common national identity," is opium for the masses, as the same rules do not apply throughout the class spectrum. Witness the writers, the politicians, the people of power, and the image of Venezuela projected to the world: there, the overwhelming majority display no African traits, although twenty percent of the population is black and another fifty percent mulatto.

Winthrop R. Wright offers a very fine analysis of the ethnic situation. He maintains that "Venezuelans do not adhere to the Anglo-Saxon belief that a drop of African blood in the veins makes an individual black. Because they stress the need to whiten their population, white Venezuelans have not condemned individuals for having some African ancestry. Rather they have rewarded the whiter citizens with greater opportunities for social improvement."[16] The emphasis is on *blanquear*, moving away from the African somatic norm toward the European; the thrust of the social pressure is to deafricanize from the bottom and miscegenate toward the top.

Wright's views on miscegenation are consistent with those of Díaz Sánchez and Sojo. He extends the argument, however, to include economics:

16. "Elitist Attitudes toward Race in Twentieth-Century Venezuela," 327. These ideas are developed to their fullest in Wright's book *Café con leche: Race, Class, and National Image in Venezuela.*

> In their own minds contemporary Venezuelans have substituted economic discrimination for racial discrimination. But the result is much the same as North American racism. Like the Yankees, Venezuelans blame economic failure on cultural and physical inferiority. They have developed a circuitous argument that states that they dislike blacks because blacks are poor; the majority of blacks are poor because they are black. Following such logic, the whiter Venezuelans refuse to consider themselves racists. They claim to discriminate for economic reasons alone. For them race remains largely a social concept, for when a black escapes poverty he or she ceases to be socially black.[17]

During the 1980s, the race/class debate was raised to a national level in an issue of the magazine *SIC* devoted to "Racismo neustro" ("Our Racism"). In an article entitled "El umbral de color" ("The Color Threshold"), Ignacio Castillo S. states: "The matter of ethnic racial relations in our society is not, in the first place, a problem of legal discrimination. It is above all a cultural problem, that is to say, a problem which manifests itself in work, consumerism, the distribution of power, the hegemony of knowledge, valuing and fantasizing."[18] The question is addressed and the answer presented more bluntly by Otto Maduro in the same issue, in his article, "Clases y razas" ("Classes and Races"):

> And nevertheless, some events seem to suggest that in present-day Venezuela there is true oppression and discrimination against blacks. How, if not, does one explain the even smaller proportion of blacks in relation as one climbs the social scale? In banks, in industry, in the army, in the clergy, in certain political parties (COPEI in particular), in the best-paid professions—in proportion, as one scans the different levels of power, one notices that the more power a given rank has, the fewer blacks there are in it.[19]

Maduro states clearly that the inverse is true concerning blacks and whites in positions of power in Venezuela—that is, the further down the ethnic scale, the darker it becomes. This situation is consistent with the position of the black population in other South American countries.

Even some literary scholars who have built parts of their reputations by studying Afro-Venezuelan culture often downplay its importance. In a series of interviews exploring "La cultura negra en Venezuela" ("Black Culture in Venezuela"), Margarita D'Amico

17. "Elitist Attitudes toward Race," 327–28.
18. Second article in the issue, "Racismo nuestro," 56.
19. Fifth article in the issue, "Racismo nuestro," 66.

questions Miguel Acosta Saignes, Federico Brito Figueroa, Juan Liscano, and José Marcial Ramos Guédez, all authorities on blacks in Venezuela. In his segment, "El aporte negro en las artes y la transculturación" ("The Black Contribution in the Arts and Transculturation"), Juan Liscano maintains that "in the poetic order, one can say that the forms, the popular poetic meter, do not have any African influence. They are classic Spanish octosyllabic verses, but on the other hand, yes, we have another important African contribution in animal stories. The character of Brer Rabbit comes from oral African folklore."[20]

José Marcial Ramos Guédez in "Testimonio de las nuevas generaciones" ("Testimony of the New Generations") observes that "the only one who we could consider as a promoter or founder who has created a serious literature with respect to blackish Venezuelan literature is Juan Pablo Sojo."[21] Ramos Guédez refers to *Drum* by Rodríguez Cárdenas as "a basic book on Afro-Venezuelan literature."

This affirmation and negation of an Afro-Venezuelan literary consciousness is an important component of this study. The push to divest Venezuelan culture of its blackness has been an ongoing process for more than a century. The four texts under discussion are responses to the situation at different moments in time.

Subsequently, the concept of Afrocentricity is fundamental to a culturalist approach to Venezuelan literature. In *The Afrocentric Idea*, Molefi Kete Asante writes: "Afrocentricity is the most complete philosophical totalization of the African being at-the-center of his or her existence. It is not merely an artistic or literary movement. Not only is it an individual or collective quest for authenticity, but it is above all the total use of method to effect psychological, political, social, cultural, and economic change."[22]

This search for the Afrocentric, that is, the search for black authenticity, in Venezuelan literature is a process that begins with Juan Pablo Sojo and culminates with Antonio Acosta Márquez. Afrocentricity treats blacks as the subjects, rather than the objects, of the literary discourse; they are at the center, rather than at the margin, of the written expression. In their writings, the four authors studied here look to Afro-Venezuelan culture, with varying degrees of awareness and profundity, for inspiration and, in some cases, positive change.

The process of deafricanization in Venezuelan culture was ad-

20. "Nuestra africanidad," 3.
21. Ibid., 4.
22. *The Afrocentric Idea*, 125.

dressed decades ago by Juan Liscano, one of the most renowned
investigators of African culture in that country:

> The black Venezuelan, as in no other country of the Americas,
> obeyed the processes of "deafricanization" and "transculturation"
> to which the eminent Brazilian africanist Arturo Ramos refers.
> This same author points out that there are three results of the pro-
> cess of "transculturation": acceptance, adaptation, or reaction,
> and he states that "there is a reaction when counter-transcultura-
> tive movements emerge because of oppression. . . ." In Venezu-
> ela, from the Declaration of Independence, there was not, in gen-
> eral, a reaction but acceptance or adaptation.[23]

What Liscano fails to mention here is that blacks in Venezuela under
the yoke of slavery had one of the most virile and rebellious systems
of maroonage in Spanish America. The activities of Afro-Venezuelan resisters to slavery and deafricanization are well documented
by Miguel Acosta Saignes in *Vida de los esclavos negros en Venezuela*
(*The Lives of Black Slaves in Venezuela*, 1967) and by Juan Pablo Sojo in
his article, "Cofradías etno-africanas en Venezuela" ("Ethno-African
Associations in Venezuela").

The concomitant abolition of slavery, coupled with the slow process
of adaptation, did not assure blacks of acceptance into Venezuelan
society on their own terms. Only through the process of miscegenation was a common ground sought in Venezuela to allay the discrimination suffered by those of African descent. Although maroonage in
its more overt form was not necessary for most Afro-Venezuelans,
cultural maroonage was and still is a positive dimension of their
experience. The handful of studies of Afro-Venezuelan music, dance,
folklore, linguistics, and literature is evidence of this reality.

In the article "Afrocentric Hermeneutics and the Rhetoric of 'Transculturación' in Black Latin American Literature," Josaphat B. Kubayanda presents some observations that are at odds with those of
Liscano but which are pertinent to this discussion. Miscegenation
and transculturation are recognized by Kubayanda as processes
often used in Latin America to take the blackness out of the national
ethos. Regardless of whether "assimilation" or "cultural parity" is
sought, the end results seem to be the same:

> It seems obvious to an African reader that the more subtle forms of
> *transculturación* and *mestizaje*, or the more brutal forms of accul-

23. "Apuntes para la investigación del negro en Venezuela: Sus instrumentos de
música," 426.

turation and assimilation, create a de-Africanization process, especially when the mobilization and distribution of power resources remain intact. In other words the critic of Black Latin American literature cannot afford to disregard the question of socio-cultural referentiality.[24]

Moving from a definition of the term *hermeneutics* as "an art of interpretation, literary or doctrinal, in which emphasis is placed on intelligibility and meaning," Kubayanda addresses the possible Afro applicability of this concept: "Afrocentric hermeneutics therefore may well be a fresh critical venture, maybe a serious adventure that can be divided into the following categories: it pits itself against the 'fallacies' and omissions in Latin American literary and social historiographies; it reclaims African orality; and reappropriates African myth and metaphysics with an unmistakable authenticity."[25] While *Drum* and *Cumboto* appear to be at the margin of black existence, *Black St. John's Eve* and *I Think Right Here Where . . . I Am* are serious attempts to reclaim African orality and reappropriate African myth and metaphysics through cultural authenticity. The hypothesis of this study is that an understanding of the impact of deafricanization on Venezuelan culture can be arrived at through comparative readings of Afrocentric and Eurocentric texts from that country. By analyzing the products of authors who write both from within and from outside of this culture, the reader is able to perceive some of the differences in validity of interpretation of the Afro-Venezuelan experience. Although *Black St. John's Eve* and *Cumboto* treat similar fictional worlds, as do *Drum* and *I Think Right Here Where . . . I Am* in verse, there are perceptible differences in the conception and exposition of the works. These differences are revealed in this study as the authors resist the process of deafricanization and the movement toward miscegenation in their worldviews while grappling with the creation of a minority discourse that embraces the culturalist concerns of Afro-Venezuelans.

24. "Afrocentric Hermeneutics and the Rhetoric of 'Transculturación,' " 227.
25. Ibid., 228.

1

Juan Pablo Sojo

Nochebuena negra:
The Essence of the Darker Brother/Sister

Juan Pablo Sojo's *Black St. John's Eve* is a tightly woven history of the Sarabia dynasty on the cocoa plantation of Pozo Frío and its environs from about 1884 to 1928. The major chronological events take place in 1918, culminating at the San Juan celebration, the Feast of St. John the Baptist. The novel begins with the plantation's consolidation of power under the leadership of don Gisberto Sarabia and ends with its ultimate downfall at the hands of Aristimuño, the local military chief, after he is spurned by don Gisberto's daughter, Consuelo. The story line is composed of the various remembrances and actions of the characters, who are either protagonists or witnesses to history: the plantation owners are makers of history, while the indentured servants are actors in a historical and socioeconomic drama over which they have no control.

Black St. John's Eve is set into motion with the arrival of Luis Pantoja, nephew of don Gisberto. Other major characters in the novel are Crisanto Marasma, the black overseer of the plantation; Pedro Marasma, Crisanto's black son who goes to the city to become acculturated and returns to Pozo Frío; Deogracia, Crisanto's daughter and the object of Luis Pantoja's desire; Lino Bembetoyo, the poet laureate of the plantation; Tereso, a social climber; Cointa, a spurned and violated woman; and Morocota, the evil *negro*. There is a strong undercurrent of irony in *Black St. John's Eve* that tempers these characters' individual aspirations and outcomes.

As the new administrator of the property, don Gisberto has perpetuated a feudal system in which plantation owners attempt to exercise total control over the financial, physical, and psychological

15

well-being of the black workers they virtually own; the blacks of Pozo Frío are bound to the land for economic reasons and exploited within the context of rising and falling prices. When Luis Pantoja arrives, he establishes repressive new wage-granting guidelines that guarantee indentured servitude for the workers. *Black St. John's Eve* thus explores the nature of the master/servant relationship, as well as questions of machismo and family stability, violence and its many ramifications, heroism and antiheroism, and the culturalist dimension of the Afro-Venezuelan experience.

The internal structure of *Black St. John's Eve* is woven around a series of triangular relationships, each of which ends in death, disappointment, or failure. For example, the romantic love that Emeterio, a black farmhand, has for Deogracia ends in his death because of the opposition of Luis Pantoja; Cointa loves Tereso, but when Tereso leaves for Caracas and returns with Ana Rafaela as his wife, Cointa is forced to contemplate suicide and falls victim to Morocota; Aristimuño declares his love for Consuelo Sarabia, but when Consuelo rejects him for Pedro Marasma, Aristimuño seeks and gets his revenge, causing the downfall of the Sarabia family; Lino Bembetoyo betrays Juana, his common-law wife, in order to marry Altagracia "officially," but when their son dies shortly after birth it is attributed to the supernatural influence of Juana. These relationships and their consequences are the factors that bring to life the characters of *Black St. John's Eve,* who are presented intact with their aspirations, frailties, and instincts for survival.

As these triangular relationships suggest, miscegenation is the primary unifying thematic motif of *Black St. John's Eve.* The mixture is tri-ethnic—black, Indian, white—with the white male *patrón* playing the dominant role. Luis Pantoja, for instance, views black women on Pozo Frío as his property. His advances toward Deogracia are initially repelled, but other women reciprocate. The *negra* Teodora meets Luis after events associated with San Pascual, a harvest festival, behind the kitchen: "Poco después llegó ella, y allí, recostándola del tucutuco, levantó sus faldas con furia y la poseyó totalmente al son de la tambora y del furruco en celo. Sagrado y desesperado rito de Cam!" (A little while later she arrived, and there, leaning her against the tree, he raised her skirts with fury and possessed her totally to the sound of the big drum and the little one in heat. Sacred and desperate rite of Ham!)[1]

Although Teodora complies, this is a symbolic rape characteristic

---

1. Juan Pablo Sojo, *Nochebuena negra,* 128. Further citations will be made parenthetically in the text.

of master/slave relationships, since her only choice is to comply. From Luis' perspective, he is satisfying a basic human/animal need without regard for the consequences while asserting himself as the owner of Teodora. He eventually marries Deogracia at Pedro's insistence, but the union is not successful, due to differences of class and other social considerations. Perhaps the grotesque fetus that Deogracia miscarries is punishment for Luis' many transgressions against black women on Pozo Frío.

Tereso's ethnic strategy is not based on the random wild-oats-sowing tactics exhibited by Luis; his actions are much more deliberate. He, like Pedro, goes to Caracas to improve himself and returns to Pozo Frío with Ana Rafaela, an Indian woman who is perceived as white by the community. In response to Pedro's query regarding his lack of interest in the beautiful Cointa, Tereso responds:

> Eso fue una simple ilusión, Pedro. Además usté comprende, el colorcito . . . Hay que mejorarlo, vale. Yo la he corrió en Caracas, y sé lo que es una buena hembra. Además hoy soy otro; me he civilizado; antes usaba alpargatas barbonas, liencillo y andaba jediondo. Ahora tú pué ve! (276)

> (That was a simple illusion, Pedro. Besides, you understand, the color thing . . . One must improve it, right. I cornered her in Caracas, and I know what a good woman is. Besides, today I am another person; I have civilized myself; before I wore ugly sandals, linen rags and walked limping. Now look at me!)

Tereso's concern for self-improvement is not just social and economic but also extends to the ethnic realm. Tereso takes a very practical approach to the all-important question of color and improving one's ethnic stock. He is swayed by the perceived necessity to deafricanize his people in order to have social value in a miscegenated society.

The relationship between Pedro and Consuelo Sarabia evolves because she is intrigued by this educated black man whom she gets to know better through the help of Deogracia, Pedro's sister. The Pedro/Consuelo affair is the inverse of the Luis/Teodora affair, since the black male is not successful in achieving his white sexual objective. After Consuelo rejects the amorous advances of Aristimuño and declares her desire for Pedro, she is forced to return to Caracas, where she marries a rich white man. The unfortunate Pedro is left with provocative memories:

> Recordó, cómo al regreso a la anochecida, poblado el eco de los retumbos del *mina*, halló a su hermana con aquel dulce men-

saje. . . . Consuelo! sus lágrimas. Su boca húmeda, tibia . . . Sus
cabellos brunos y frescos desgajados entre sus manos . . . Ah! . . .
y contra su pecho sus senos palpitantes, su cuerpo envuelto en
calurosa fragancia de claveles recién cortados. (306)

(He remembered, as nightfall returned, populated with the echo
of the rolls of the *mina*, how he found his sister with that sweet
message. . . . Consuelo! Her tears. Her moist mouth, warm . . .
Her slick, fresh hair flowing through his hands. Oh yes! . . . and
against his chest her palpitating breasts, her body wrapped in the
warm fragrance of recently cut carnations.)

In comparing these two intimate scenes, it is apparent that the
Luis/Teodora encounter is constructed around images of violence
associated with rape and degradation. The environment created for
Pedro and Consuelo is romantic and reciprocal: Consuelo is an object of worship while Teodora is a momentary possession. There is
no evidence that a sexual union between Consuelo and Pedro is
consummated; instead, he is left in the pining stage as the novel
ends. Nor is there any other sexual union between a black man and
a white woman in *Black St. John's Eve.* Miscegenation, due to the
patriarchal structure, is a one-way street, controlled and dominated
by the white male progenitor. As a man who has undergone some of
the ritualistic, initiatory experiences of the traditional hero, one
would expect Pedro to win the princess in the end. He is not so
fortunate, however, due primarily to his blackness, which exacerbates his economic and social conditions.

The Afrocentric Worldview of
Black St. John's Eve

Orality and the "Anthropocentric Ontology"

Due to Juan Pablo Sojo's culturalist focus and the uniqueness of
his literary creation, *Black St. John's Eve* has received much more
attention as folklore and anthropology than as a work of fiction.
Guillermo Meneses addresses the problem Sojo creates for the critics when he observes, "It is possible that his closest influences,
above all in his first literary efforts and, especially, those of *Black St.
John's Eve,* cannot be found in any illustrious name of Venezuelan or
universal literature. . . . The important thing is that Juan Pablo Sojo
wrote admirable pages, filled with marvelous wisdom, precisely

because he did not have literary wisdom."[2] These remarks attest both to Juan Pablo Sojo's originality and his *difference*. He was not steeped in the literary tradition of the Venezuelan masters of the canon but instead was immersed in the traditions of orality and Afro-Venezuelan culture propagated by his father, Juan Pablo Sojo, Sr. Therefore, Juan Pablo Sojo was able to combine form and content in a unique fashion to produce the first Afrocentric novel of Spanish America.

In the section of Josaphat B. Kubayanda's "Afrocentric Hermeneutics and the Rhetoric of 'Transculturación'" devoted to "orality," he comments regarding maroon societies and language development in Colombia, Ecuador, and Puerto Rico:

> Historically, these Afro-Hispanics have had to modify and re[-]create the Spanish language; their African tongues or those of their parents inspired that linguistic transformation. The black Latin American novel and short story, for instance, contain certain elements of the traditional African epic forms, the rhetoric of parody and proverb, the structures of rhythm, and other oral narrative or poetic formulae.[3]

The narrative discourse of *Black St. John's Eve* contains several important elements relating to the African oral tradition, including the memorization and re-creation of historical events from various perspectives, the utilization of proverbs and stories for humorous and didactic purposes, the rhythmic structures of the drum culture, and the use of literary intertextuality to underscore cultural cohesiveness. It is through the imaginative use of language that the novel's Afrocentric worldview is sustained.

Regarding African linguistic remnants in Venezuela, Max Hans Brandt, who is skeptical of the impact of African languages upon Venezuelan Spanish, sees minimal influence:

> At least ten words of apparent African origin are still used in Barlovento including the following: *Kitimba* (a drum), *Kichimba* (a drumming style), *malembe* (a type of music and adjective describing San Juan—Saint John the Baptist), *guaricongo* (another adjective describing San Juan), *Birongo* (a village name), *Ganga* (another village close to *Birongo*), *Cafunga* (a type of food), and *camukenge* (a small animal).[4]

2. "Veinticinco años de novela venezolana," 216.
3. "Afrocentric Hermeneutics and the Rhetoric of 'Transculturación' in Black Latin American Literature," 230–31.
4. "An Ethnomusicological Study of Three Afro-Venezuelan Drum Ensembles of Barlovento." Chapter 1, "Barlovento and the Background for Research," 5–17, is especially informative.

These lexical items are important in a work of literature only to the degree that they are incorporated meaningfully into its structure. The Afrocentric focus of *Black St. John's Eve* is based upon more subtle narrative strategies. This point is driven home by William W. Megenney, who conducts an extensive analysis of African linguistic elements in *Black St. John's Eve* and demonstrates how they relate to the novel's worldview.[5] Megenney discusses the origins of such words as *tolole, cachimbo, Mandinga, cafunga, malembe, dengue, perren-dengue, lembe,* and *mina,* for example, to show how they are used as cultural identity markers in the novel. These words have survived linguistic transformation and extinction by the dominant language to remain viable components of oral and written expression.

In the discussion of "myth and metaphysics," while referring to "ancestral agents," Kubayanda asserts that "Pedro, in Juan Pablo Sojo's novel, *Black St. John's Eve,* lives by the moral tenets that have been passed on to him by his father, Crisanto Marasma. Crisanto is the oral historiographer, the Hispanicized *griot* [oral historian] of Barlovento, the moral conscience of an oral people."[6] Crisanto's function is made clear early in the novel:

> Ninguno en Barlovento, conocía más historias que Crisanto Ma-rasma. Por su imaginación pasaban los nombres de todos los na-tivos y forasteros residenciados en aquellas tierras, con sus vir-tudes y miserias. . . . El solo comprendía el dolor mudo y trágico de todos aquellos brazos incansables, de aquellos rostros dema-crados, de aquellos ojos asombrados llenos de miedo y supersti-ción. (73–74)

> (Nobody in Barlovento knew more life stories than Crisanto Ma-rasma. Through his imagination flowed the names of all the na-tives and strangers residing in those lands, with their virtues and miseries. . . . He alone understood the deaf and tragic pain of those tireless limbs, of those abused faces, of those wide eyes filled with fear and superstition.)

In his capacity as *griot,* Crisanto Marasma structures most of *Black St. John's Eve* through his subjective mixture of fact and fantasy, truth and lie. It is he who weaves the unofficial history of Barlo-vento and the happenings within the closed environment of Pozo

5. "Africa en Venezuela: Su herencia lingüística y su cultura literaria," 207–60. The list of terms compiled by Juan Pablo Sojo, however, "Material para un glosario de afro-negrismos de Venezuela" ("Material for a Glossary of Afro-Negrisms of Vene-zuela"), remains the most authoritative source for an understanding of African influ-ences in Venezuelan Spanish.

6. "Afrocentric Hermeneutics and the Rhetoric of 'Transculturación,' " 234.

Frío. He bears witness to the sufferings and achievements of the workers through knowledge, imagination, thoughts, and remembrances. A female perspective to events is given by Regana, the domestic, who along with Crisanto has served the Sarabias since 1884. It is she who tells Crisanto's story.

At the end of *Black St. John's Eve* there is the suggestion that Pedro will carry on the tradition of oral historian of Pozo Frío. Ten years have transpired since the climactic events of the San Juan celebration of 1918. Crisanto is dead, the Sarabia dynasty exists no more, and other major characters have faded into the background. Pedro realizes that no profound structural changes have occurred:

> Ahora recorría de nuevo los viejos caminos, aquellos hondones del recuerdo perdidos entre las ruinas de los ranchos y de los pueblos abandonados. Allí, en la paz de las haciendas, los hijos de la tierra seguían gibados bajo los sacos; bregando de sol a sol sobre los barbacoales rebeldes; alegrando sus vidas oscuras con aguardiente y tambor. La fulia en la boca de las mujeres, y el *mina*, y el carangano, y el cuatro y la "grande," no dejaron de cantar como no dejan de correr y cantar el río y los pájaros. Y aun sobrará tiempo para darle el último beso a la tierra. (311)

> (Now he recrossed again the old roads, those deep recesses of lost memory among the ruins of the shacks and abandoned towns. There in the peace of the ranches, the children of the earth remained bent over by the bags; struggling from sun up to sun down in the rebellious fields; lighting up their dark lives with liquor and the drum. The song in the mouths of the women, and the *mina*, the *carangano*, and the *cuatro* and the "*grande*" did not stop singing just as the flowing of the river and the singing of the birds did not stop. And yet more than enough time remained to give to the earth that last kiss.)

Across generations, the situation of neocolonialism will be perpetrated with the only real freedom for Afro-Venezuelans being perhaps in their own thoughts. Pedro is important, just as his father was before him, because he is the repository of the collective memory of this populace with the responsibility of assuring that their story is told and retold for generations to come.

Like many other Afrocentric works, *Black St. John's Eve* has its "anthropocentric ontology," which John Mbiti defines as being so "in the sense everything is seen in terms of its relation to man." Among the five categories of ontological phenomena Mbiti outlines is "Animals and plants, or the remainder of biological life." These phenomena and objects "constitute the environment in which man lives, provide a means of existence and, if need be, man establishes a mystical relationship with them."[7] The ever-present Tuy River is illustrative of Mbiti's concepts: "Because the Tuy has that; it is a sovereign who demands its tribute and obtains it. When it is not a caiman, it is the roots similar to gigantic tentacles strangling the already inert bodies in the depths of the pools. . . . It is possible that in the water of this river lives alert underwater vegetation of anthropomorphagous trees."[8] The Tuy River commands respect from and instills fear in the populace. Much of the human drama in Pozo Frío is played out against the backdrop of this natural phenomenon that gives and takes away life while providing spiritual inspiration. During the rainy season, "los caños se hinchan y el Tuy engruesa repicando sus cien *minas* milenarios" (the canes sink and the swelling Tuy resounds its one hundred millennium drums; 178). Always in tune with human sentiments, a component of a metaphorical environment, the Tuy's reaction when Cointa is betrayed by Tereso for Ana Rafaela mirrors the anguish of the distraught victim:

> Allí cerca comenzaba el Tuy a rugir. Era el estremecimiento de cien tambores tocados por Mandinga; el redoble de las *minas* infernales que sonaban enfurecidos, a cuyo toque bailaban las sombras de los malos amos, aquellos que azotaron las carnes indefensas de los esclavos buenos. (188)

> (Near here the Tuy began to roar. It was the trembling of a hundred drums beaten by Mandinga; the drum roll of the hellish *minas* which resounded infuriated, to whose sound the shadows of the evil owners danced, those who beat the defenseless flesh of the good slaves.)

In this instance, the Tuy becomes a metaphor for the death and suffering that has occurred among the black population from slavery to the present. The drums and music echoed in this scene are far removed from the ritualistic, celebratory patterns performed during important events. The Tuy's reaction presages impending doom. Throughout the novel, the river is seen in terms of its relationship to humans and, indeed, forms part of a mystical relationship with them in an Afro-ontological sense.

---

7. *African Religions and Philosophy,* 15–28. The five categories are: 1. God as the ultimate explanation of the genesis and sustenance of both man and all things; 2. Spirits being made up of superhuman beings and the spirits of men who died a long time ago; 3. Man, including human beings who are alive and those about to be born; 4. Animals and plants, or the remainder of biological life; 5. Phenomena and objects without biological life (16).

8. *African Religions and Philosophy,* 117.

Violence, Magical Realism, and the Mampulorio

Both psychological and physical violence are important motifs in the development of *Black St. John's Eve*. The plantation owners are the classic perpetrators of psychological violence, the manifestations of which vary from Luis Pantoja's wage-granting rules to the exploitative economic practices of don Gisberto Sarabia against Viviano Blanco and of Doctor Goyo against Reyes Mota. Blanco and Mota are treated as "equals" while they are placed in untenable financial positions and their property is taken away. They both end "muerto boca abajo" (dead face down) as a result of their victimization.

There is also a certain amount of random, in-group, horizontal violence at work on Pozo Frío, which takes place during fiestas and is evidenced through fights, threats, and insults. The most violent act of this group of blacks is the brutal rape of Cointa by Morocota; Morocota, as we will see later, receives divine punishment for this crime. Ironically, in spite of all the ruminations and words of Crisanto and Pedro Marasma, neither does anything overtly to change the system. The only act of vertical violence committed against the masters is carried out by Guaraco, an Indian, who executes Doctor Goyo to put an end to his exploitative practices. Indeed, revenge is yet another consistent motif in *Black St. John's Eve* and serves to accentuate the problematic relationships between rich and poor.

There is thus both veiled and overt criticism of the powerful in *Black St. John's Eve* as the characters' stories unfold beneath the oppression wielded by the colonial structures, especially the oligarchy, the military, and the church. *Black St. John's Eve* brings into clear focus the far-reaching impact these three repressive forces have upon the sexual, economic, and social lives of the poor blacks, mulattoes, and mestizos who populate the novel. The overt signs of dissent range from the novel's representation of the various schemes used to manipulate blacks out of their property by the Sarabias, Goyos, Aristimuños, and Zappas to its representation of the forced recruitment of men to fight the unpopular wars of the dictator Juan Vicente Gómez.

The episode devoted to Morocota is characterized by sex and violence, with qualities of both the magical and the real. It is magical to the degree that the reader is confronted with a series of events based on fantasy and horror that defy the logical imagination. Morocota's plight is real in that it evolves out of a set of common cultural beliefs held by the blacks of Barlovento. The situation is described as "satanic anthropomorphism" by Pedro Lhaya.[9]

9. *Juan Pablo Sojo: Pasión y acento de su tierra*, 96.

Morocota the *pagay* (boat pilot) rapes Cointa and must pay for his despicable acts. Aunt Iginia condemns him: "—Negro singón! . . . No vaj a podé comé por tu mano! . . . Dios s'ta arriba!" (—Shameless nigger! . . . You ain't gonna be able to eat with your hands! . . . God is still on the throne!; 256). The condemnation of Morocota takes place within the ritualistic dimension of a natural metaphoric environment and the drum culture of death. His act is denounced by frogs, the river, monkeys, and the drums of Hell.

Unexpectedly, the fierce, intimidating Morocota begins to suffer hallucinations and is visited by "El Aruco," which is described as an "ave fabulosa de la montaña que los campesinos tienen como encarnación misma de los espiritus infernales. Dicen que quien la oye cantar, queda loco" (fabulous mountain bird which the country people take for the very incarnation of hellish spirits. They say that whoever hears it sing, goes crazy; 314). Morocota is faced with a set of circumstances that defies logical explanation as he escapes into fear and madness caused by the presence of the Aruco.

In his mind, Morocota kills the hellish Aruco, plucks it, cooks it, eats it, and defecates, but the bird leaves his body flying and talking to him. As a result of his mental condition, Morocota, *patuleco* (disoriented), is last observed in a state of disrepair: "Parecía que un destello de cordura le volvía. Se mesaba el cabello crecido y esponjado; babeaba, llorando como una mujer" (It seemed like a beam of wisdom turned him. He pulled out his long and nappy hair, foamed at the mouth, crying like a woman; 291). The spell that Aunt Iginia places upon Morocota is effective because he believes in the powers of the demons she invokes and therefore suffers the consequences. In the final analysis, the reader is presented with an outstanding example of what is commonly called "realismo mágico" (magical realism) from a black perspective.

In his attempt to arrive at a coherent definition of this term, Luis Leal discusses its differences from fantastic, psychological, surrealist, and hermetic literatures; he then explains:

> Magical Realism is not a major literature either. Its objective is not, as is that of magic, the stirring up of emotions, but the expressing of them. Magical Realism is, more than anything, an attitude toward reality, which can be expressed in popular or learned forms, in sophisticated or plain styles, in closed or open structures. What is the attitude of the magical realist toward reality? We have already stated they do not create imaginary worlds in which we might be able to take refuge to avoid daily reality. In Magical Realism the author confronts reality and tries to unravel it, by

discovering what there is of mystery in things, in life, in human actions.[10]

In the Morocota episode there is neither a psychological evaluation of him nor a disfiguration of reality nor a creation of imagined worlds. There is, however, an attitude toward reality expressed in popular form through a folk-based worldview which allows the author to interpret the mysteries of Afro-Venezuelan life and its relationship to the cosmos in Barlovento. "In Magical Realism the key events do not have a logical or psychological explanation," writes Leal.[11] This magical presentation of events is an outgrowth of the popular culture of the region rather than a logical explanation of a set of inexplicable circumstances.

A similar episode of magical realism occurs in the case of "el Matacán," a deer whom hunters like Lino Bembetoyo believe is the reincarnation of Mandinga, the Devil himself. The story is told to Crisanto by Lino as they await the arrival of Luis Pantoja and scheme on how to deal with him. Matacán has left an indelible mark on the hunter's psyche: "Mire viejo! La jedentina azufre que nos dejó, hizo juir los perros rabo entre piernas, y a nosotros nos puso a rezá cuanto sabíamos!" (Look partner! The stinking brimstone it left us made the dogs bolt with their tails between their legs and made us pray as much as we knew how!; 38) The Matacán figure is very prevalent in the popular imagination of this region. As such, its appearance is accepted as an attempt to bridge the gap between fantasy and reality in the popular mentality during these magically real episodes.

There is some disagreement among critics regarding the manifestations of concepts such as *negritud* and *realismo mágico* in Afro-Hispanic and indigenous literatures in Spanish America. Horst Rogmann views these tendencies as European impositions that are used by the writers to combat the inferiority they feel at being unable to compete with the standards of world-class authors. Citing the Guatemalan Miguel Angel Asturias as an example of magical realist tendencies, Rogmann writes that "this consists, within his literary creation, primarily of utilizing mythic elements such as witches, shamanism, the god Tohil, the mixture of realist and dreamlike elements which supposedly is an expression of indigenous thought, and a magical conception of the Word and its bard the poet, also derived from indigenous tradition."[12] These are cultur-

10. "El realismo mágico en la literatura hispanoamericana," 232–33.
11. Ibid., 234.
12. "Realismo mágico y 'negritud' como construcciones ideológicas," 46.

alist characteristics of Asturias's works that are based upon his learned knowledge of indigenous myths and legends. This content, of course, is what makes the literature Guatemalan and not German.

After asserting that the Europeans also invented *negritud*, although Africans applied the concept, Rogmann explains: "Among its themes, attention is called to the importance given to sexuality, physiology, musicality, and black dances, in addition to the ancestors' cult."[13] As interesting and polemical as this article is, Rogmann does not cite any Afrocentric texts written by blacks from South America to buttress his arguments. Nevertheless, manifestations of both magical realism and *negritud* form the core of *Black St. John's Eve*, precisely because they evolve out of the internal dynamics of the work regarding Afro-Venezuelan culture and are not externally imposed categories.

Related closely to the concept of magical realism in Afro-Venezuelan culture is what Alfredo Chacón labels "magical religious activity": "When it is designated as magical-religious, this means that the representations and beliefs, as well as the acts through which they are placed, in effect show in their makeup magical and religious aspects mixed together; but at the same time it means that in this mixture magical and religious specificity is not lost."[14] Specifically, the magical aspect is related to extrahuman and extranatural powers that are used by practitioners and believers to have the desired positive or negative impact upon their target. Whereas in the Morocota episode magical activity is channeled in the direction of revenge and punishment, there is a more benign dimension to these activities. The Mampulorio, a religious practice prevalent in this novel, exemplifies a cohesive mixture of religious and magical activity. Pedro Lhaya describes the Mampulorio as "the wake of an infant, with a description of the preparation of the dead child, and the accompanying celebration while the mother mourns. (A custom which has disappeared.)"[15] The custom of having a wake for the dead has not disappeared, but perhaps the name has changed. In *Black St. John's Eve* more attention is devoted to fictionalizing the ritualistic atmosphere surrounding the ceremony than to describing intricate anthropological details. The overall meaning of the Mampulorio is more complex than what Lhaya suggests, however.

The Mampulorio is a ceremony devoted to a dead child that is designed to ease the transition from the physical to the spiritual

13. Ibid., 48.
14. *Poblaciones y culturas negras de Venezuela*, 62.
15. *Juan Pablo Sojo*, 119–20.

world.[16] In *Black St. John's Eve* it is enacted after the death of the newly born Timoteo Bermúdez to his parents, Lino and Altagracia. This particular episode takes place against a backdrop of ethnic tension occasioned by the return from Caracas of Tereso and Ana Rafaela to the house of Tereso's mother, Celedonia. Ironically, Cointa, who is jealous of Ana, and Morocota, who is jealous of Tereso, use the occasion of this gathering to humiliate the newly returned couple.

Within the cultural practice of the Mampulorio, there are many folk beliefs, ranging from the cries of the birds of evil omen to the act of administering folk treatments to the child before and after he dies. During the festivities, ritualistic drinking and dancing predominate:

> Por las ánimas benditas
> que están en el Purgatorio
> apaga la vela del mampulorio!
> Apaga la vela
> del mampulorio!
> (232–33)

> (For the blessed souls
> that are in Purgatory
> extinguish the candle of the Mampulorio!
> Extinguish the candle
> of the Mampulorio!)

This is an occasion for the reaffirmation of life rather than the acceptance of death by the people. The intertextual dimension of the Mampulorio is demonstrated in Sojo's poem "Elegía del niño muerto" ("Elegy of the Dead Child"), which also captures the spirit of the dialectical tension between life and death:

> Se murió la nochebuena de San Juan!
> Como en la vela la llama
> se apagó su vida buena . . .
> Era una estrellita blanca
> siendo su piel tan morena,
> Se murió la nochebuena de San Juan![17]

16. According to Benjamín Núñez, the Mampulorio is "in Venezuela and the Antilles, an elaborate ceremony involving song and dance rituals; performed by blacks upon the death of a child." *Dictionary of Afro-Latin American Civilization*, 294–95.
17. Lhaya, *Juan Pablo Sojo*, 119–20.

(He died on St. John's Eve
Like the flame of the candle
His good life was snuffed out . . .
He was a little white star
Having such brown skin
He died on St. John's Eve!)

The version of the Mampulorio that has been introduced into the official folklore of Venezuela is very different from the ceremony poeticized and interpreted by Juan Pablo Sojo in *Black St. John's Eve*. In *El Mampulorio*, a musical version of the ceremony with melody by Juan Liscano and harmony by Isabel Aretz, the Mampulorio is presented as a children's game replete with music and dance. In the introduction to their presentation, the authors state: "The first mention that we know of this dance is owed to the poet and researcher Juan Liscano, who copied the music and some facts about the Mampulorio in Curiepe."[18] *Black St. John's Eve*, written in 1930 and published in 1943, contains the first written description of this ceremony, and Sojo's "Elegy of the Dead Child: The Mampulorio" is also an interpretation of the celebration associated with a child's death as we have observed. Therefore, Sojo and not Liscano should be credited with being the source of this black, folk-based ritual.

However, which version came first is not the primary issue. From the perspective of deafricanization, it is interesting that much of Afro-Venezuelan culture has been reinterpreted, restructured into the national *criollo* framework, and lost in the process. The Mampulorio is but one example of how this happens. Luis Felipe Ramón y Rivera writes regarding this dance: "Choreographically, it is possible that said dance had some or much African. Musically it has very little: alternate responses and short clichés in both the solo and choral parts. The rhythm of the melody and its accompaniment is the same as the merengue, that is, a rhythm which is the product of several mixtures, not specifically africanish."[19] This is the "official" version of the transformation of an Afro-Venezuelan ritual into a "national" product.

Cultural Syncretism and the Slave Culture

The events of June 24, 1918—the celebration of the Feast of Saint John the Baptist—is the climax of *Black St. John's Eve*. Sojo inter-

18. *El Mampulorio*, 4.
19. *La música afrovenezolana*, 93.

prets this ceremony as a celebration of cultural syncretism, both religious and secular. Regarding the Feast of Saint John the Baptist in Venezuela, Juan Liscano has written:

> In Venezuela, among the blacks, the celebration of the Feast of St. John lost almost entirely its religious inspiration to saturate itself with the rhythmicity of orgiastic power and energetic drunkedness. Through that discharge of social vitality, of the display of extroversion and ritual communication, there is reached without a doubt through depersonalization, an identification with supernatural presences.[20]

In Venezuela, on June 24, the word *Nochebuena* (Christmas Eve) refers to the Eve of Saint John the Baptist's celebration, not to Christmas Eve as in December. The rituals involve proper respect for the Catholic religion and to the cult of Saint John the Baptist.

While Saint John is ostensibly the focus of these activities of the celebration, the ritual takes on that air of rhythmicity, orgiastic power, and uncontrolled energy mentioned by Liscano in an effort to try and answer the ancestral call from Africa:

> People came from everywhere. Dancers and spectators meshed together without knowing how. Suddenly their feet began to dance and the dancers were now those who looked at the others when they felt tired. The great voice of the old *mina*! The voice of the ancestor congregating the clan! A mysterious voice, which reclaims its African blood, the remainder of African blood lost in the recesses of the veins like a vague reminiscence![21]

The supernatural presence with which they identify is stimulated by the *mina*, whose toll links African and Afro-Venezuelan experiences through rhythmic expression to "pay homage to the great voice which came from the ancestor." This drum is one of the primary internal structural motifs of the novel. What begins as a homage to a traditional Christian saint culminates in a manifestation of subconscious ancestral yearnings. As such, it is a powerful and effective example of religious syncretism based in Afro-Venezuelan cultural myths.

Several other Afrocentric rituals in *Black St. John's Eve* have their basis in slave culture and provide the mythic basis of the Barlovento worldview. These include superstitions associated with La Sayona and El Hermano Penitente, witchcraft/spiritualism, the Mampu-

20. *La Fiesta de San Juan el Bautista*, 47.
21. Ibid., 299–300.

lorio, as well as the parables associated with Tío Conejo and other animals. It is Lino Bembetoyo, the popular teller of tales, who brings alive the Brer Rabbit stories—usually to serve to his advantage. Lino relates how through his guile, Brer Rabbit is able to imprison the wasp and the snake and bring a crocodile tear to God in an effort to be made larger. God denies his request by rationalizing that if Brer Rabbit is so effective as small as he is, what chance would the others have if the rabbit were bigger? Lino's motive for this particular tale is that Guaraco, who is in the audience, is aware that Juana, his sister, is about to be deceived by Lino, who seeks the favors of Altagracia. Thus, Lino ends his story: "Por eso no hay que fiarse ni de conejo, ni de indio!" (For that reason one cannot trust either a rabbit nor an Indian; 54). This attack upon Guaraco's credibility draws a threatening response from him, but in the end the episode is treated as good fun.

These animal stories represent an important aspect of the collective memory not only of Afro-Venezuelans but also of most New World blacks. Miguel Acosta Saignes observes that

> the stories of Brer Tiger and Brer Rabbit have been nothing more than prolongations of African narrations in America; they arrived to our days, by word of mouth from the slaves, from memory to memory of the freed, from remembrance to remembrance of "black nannies," from countryside to countryside and from city to city. The old educational and explanatory stories of the life of the African world crossed the ocean and assumed among us the incarnations of Brer Rabbit and Brer Tiger.[22]

Brer Rabbit, in particular, due to his guile and cunning, was used by the slaves to outwit the master on a symbolic level, a psychological process which has been passed on through the centuries to resist domination by the oppressor. Brer Rabbit represents the epitome of cultural maroonage, a combination of the supernatural and the social which helped to mitigate the adverse circumstances under which blacks have struggled. In this particular instance, and others, Lino goes back in time to "when the animals spoke" to fabricate stories that serve in his own interest but that nevertheless follow a pattern familiar to his audience based upon ancestral patterns. Thus Lino's function as teller of tales is just as important as the role of Crisanto as *griot*—they both reinforce black collective memory.

Acosta Saignes states in another observation regarding slave culture: "The slaves were always immersed in legend, witchcraft, myth, and from their fabulous world they projected upon the owner's uni-

---

22. *Vida de los esclavos negros en Venezuela,* 190.

verse beliefs and superstitions, procedures to promote happiness, which in the blacks was only the anxiety for liberty, and for the owners licentiousness; methods to evoke evil powers and certain gods whose origin neither the descendants of the Africans nor their owners knew but who they began to accept as infallible."[23]

This mythic world the slaves created survived temporal and spatial limitations to become an important cultural element for freedom and survival. The Afrocentric, magical-realist worldview of *Black St. John's Eve* is imbued with manifestations of legends like La Sayona and El Hermano Penitente, inexplicable happenings that the people attribute to witchcraft, evil omens incarnated in birds and snakes, and a basic attempt by blacks to create an alternative method for viewing and understanding the world in which they live. The novel demonstrates clearly an attempt to escape intolerable social and economic circumstances through the creation of Afro-Venezuelan spiritual and psychological alternatives.

Finally, there is a racist attitudinal structure in *Black St. John's Eve* that is perpetrated by those in power, including Luis Pantoja, Colonel Aristimuño, don Gisberto Sarabia, Doctor Goyo, Musiú Zappa, and the church representative. The oligarchy, the military, and the church do what is necessary to keep the black workers poor and ignorant. Luis Pantoja, the principal practitioner of racial superiority, believes that black men are innately violent and bloodthirsty, while black women are sexual objects. His further comments speak of black genetic inferiority in comparison to Yankees and Europeans. This mindset underscores the ruling class's attitude toward Afro-Venezuelans. They are there to serve the needs of the owners, to be exploited at will, deemed inferior and unworthy of advancement, and cast aside. The social irony of *Black St. John's Eve* is that neither money nor education alters the negative perceptions of Afro-Venezuelans held by their white compatriots. This is the lesson Tereso has learned all too well: being civilized is not enough. That is, deafricanization at the most elemental biological level appears to be the only way to change the social structures.

Black St. John's Eve, penned in 1930 but published in 1943, still remains the most viable Afro-Venezuelan novel precisely because of the mixture of culturalist elements it contains. It is a fictional evaluation of the Barlovento region focusing upon ethnic memory, myth, time, and the private lives of blacks. Juan Pablo Sojo moves this population from the periphery to the center of the Venezuelan cultural ethos as subjects, rather than objects.

23. Ibid., 188.

Although *Black St. John's Eve* has been praised for its cultural authenticity regarding the African dimension of Venezuelan society, Max Hans Brandt maintains that much of the factual information presented by Sojo in his essays and later fictionalized is not reliable. Be that as it may, this novel is a work of fiction whose overall meaning is enhanced through the dynamic interplay between the real and imagined worlds. The main issues regarding deafricanization and miscegenation, the focus of this study, are brought into clearer focus through Sojo's interpretation of reality.

2

Ramón Díaz Sánchez

Cumboto:
Let Us All Miscegenate

Of the works analyzed in this study, *Cumboto* has received the most critical scrutiny, due primarily to the reputation of its author. Regarding *Cumboto*, Kessel Schwartz, the literary historian, writes that

> it is a sober projection and psychological exploration of the Negro soul and the problems of mestizaje. The novelist studies black and white relationships on a coconut hacienda near Puerto Cabello, where he spent his youth. The protest against the customs of the coastal town is less important than the dream-like mixture of present and past, portrayals of psyches, both black and white, superstition, terror, magic symbolism, and fantasy which fill the novel.[1]

These comments by Schwartz touch upon some of the basic features of *Cumboto* while praising it as an outstanding work of fiction. In her summary of *Cumboto*, Shirley M. Jackson states:

> Through the emotional eyes of the old black slave Natividad, the novel *Cumboto* (which means with boats) presents Venezuelan reality in a remembrance of the days of his youth. The black outlines the epic of Venezuela, epitome of all America. He re-creates the life of the black African and their mulatto descendants from the first tragic steps that anticipated the institution of slavery, until the end of that era, to the growing up of the mulatto son, the new owner of the remaining properties.[2]

1. *A New History of Spanish-American Fiction*, 74.
2. *La novela negrista en hispanoamerica*, 40.

Cumboto assesses the postslavery period of the region while bring-
ing into clearer focus the relationships of blacks to the white power
structure which continues to dominate their lives, as if no progress
had been made.

The novel consists of one giant flashback from the perspective of
Natividad, the narrator. The flashback is triggered by the arrival of a
stranger to the plantation Cumboto who requests to see Federico,
the present owner. This stranger, who turns out to be a product of
Federico's sexual union with a black woman, Pascua, is interpreted
by Natividad as the future leader of Cumboto. The chronological
sequence of *Cumboto* transpires over a period of hours, but the psychological or human time stretches from the founding of Cumboto
by maroons to the present, embracing most of the nineteenth and
early twentieth centuries.

According to the history given in the novel, the white Arguíndegui family originally settled and owned Cumboto, but they were
bought out by the Lamarca family in 1853. Subsequently, the white
owners of Cumboto are Lamarcas while some of the former slave
families retain the Arguíndegui name. Mamerto, the grandfather of
the character Abuela Anita, was one of the slaves who maintained
the Arguíndegui name, thus carrying it on to this generation.

The primary characters are Guillermo and Beatriz Lamarca, the
past owners of Cumboto; their son, Federico; Frau Berza, the white
female piano teacher who carries on a secret sexual liaison with
Cruz María, a mulatto; Abuela Anita, a black descendant of slaves,
who knows most of the region's history; Abuela's daughter, Pascua;
Abuela's grandson, Fernando Arguíndegui, who traces his heritage
to the original white founders of the settlement; Venancio, the keeper
of the oral tradition; and Cervelión, who accepts Natividad when he
is expelled from the White House by Guillermo. The lives of these
characters are inextricably bound by the economic and biological
exigencies of Cumboto. Their private lives are narrated to the reader
through the subjectivity of Natividad, who has the privilege of leaving out as much as he tells.

Natividad, the narrator/witness/protagonist, is an enigma, to say
the least. He characterizes himself as Federico's "shadow," an insig-
nificant other who is a victim of history. Natividad has no identity
because he exists only as an idea, an abstraction of what blacks
should be in the white supremacist ideology of Cumboto. He is
therefore portrayed in the novel as a rootless, intraethnic voyager
who is projected by the author as a historical informant.

Critics point out the fact that Federico is Natividad's alter ego, his
shadow, but Natividad sees his role as being much more important:

"me afirmaba en la idea de que era esto lo que faltaba al hijo de don Guillermo para penetrar en la entraña viviente de este universo: una segunda conciencia, una conciencia negra. He aquí mi papel" (I convinced myself of the idea that that was what Guillermo's son lacked in order to penetrate into the living center of this universe: a second conscience, a black conscience. This is my role).[3] In this role he becomes an ethnic cheerleader, a culture pimp who must help Federico bridge the gap between European and African cultures. Natividad is the typical "house nigger" who is impressed with his self-importance.

The first part of *Cumboto*, "Un mundo encantado" ("An Enchanted World"), is narrated from the perspective of Natividad as he recounts childhood episodes with Federico and Federico's sister Gertrudis that have left impressions upon him. From the initial encounter with the stranger in the afternoon of the present, an encompassing flashback treats the founding of Cumboto, the characteristics of its owners and inhabitants, the secret relationship between Frau Berza and Cruz María, and the wonderful and magical world of Abuela Anita. Abuela Anita is a repository of history and represents the collective ethnic memory of blacks. As we learn at the end of the novel, the trunk that she inherits from her grandfather, Mamerto, is a virtual Pandora's box of Cumboto's *intrahistoria*.

The narrator says of Abuela Anita that "su figura tenía un aire de fetiche africano" (her body had the presence of an African fetish; 52), and her color is "negra retinta, absoluta" (absolutely blue black; 51). Abuela Anita is steeped in the popular myths of Cumboto and its environs:

> Familiares le eran todos los fantasmagóricos personajes que infestaban el mundo de los negros y que se meten en las alcobas, se apoderan de los hogares, pululan en los suburbios de las ciudades y hacen de las iglesias y los cementerios lugares de pavor. La Mula maneada, el Carretón, la Sayona, las Animas del Purgatorio, los difuntos atormentados que arrastraban cadenas más allá de la tumba y los infelices que habiendo enterrado en vida su dinero penan después de muertos hasta que algún alma piadosa los desentierra y los saca de pena con unas misas. (53)

> (Familiar to her were all the phantasmagoric characters who infested the world of the blacks and who are present in the bedrooms, take over the households, swarm in the suburbs of the city, and make the churches and the cemeteries places of fear. The Hob-

---

3. Ramón Díaz Sánchez, *Cumboto*, 159. Further citations will be made parenthetically in the text.

bled Mule, the *Carretón*, the Sayona, the Souls of Purgatory, the
tormented dead who drag chains away from the tomb, and the
unfortunates, who having buried their money in life, suffer after
death until some merciful soul unearths them and takes them out
of their misery with a few masses.)

Compared to those of the characters of *Black St. John's Eve*, Abuela
Anita's interpretations are external, descriptive projections of black
myth rather than active attempts to incorporate known African
mythic practices into different manifestations of Afro-Venezuelan
culture. Folk beliefs are prevalent in both novels but remain on the
periphery of *Cumboto* instead of being functional components of the
black ethos.

"La huella de Satanás" ("Satan's Trail"), the second part of *Cumboto*,
is structured around images of madness and death: doña Beatriz Lamarca, who is suspected to have had an affair with Jaime
Rojas, her mulatto piano teacher, emerges from the seclusion of her
room to act out episodes of her romantic past with a general who
had deceived her thirty years before; Natividad undergoes sexual
initiation with Pastora; Cruz María is shot and killed by don Guillermo during one of his late-night encounters with Frau Berza; Federico and Gertrudis leave for Europe; Natividad is expelled from the
White House by don Guillermo and is taken in by Cervelión, coming face to face with black culture; Abuela Anita indoctrinates Natividad in Arguíndegui family history; Cervelión and other blacks
conspire to revenge Cruz María, apparently using ritual to influence don Guillermo's death from snakebite.

Natividad's initial reaction to black culture is one of shock: "Jamás
me acostumbraría a semejante vida ni me sentiría unido espiritual-
mente a aquellos seres estúpidos y socarrones que no sabían hablar
sino de miserias" (I would never become accustomed to such a life
nor would I feel spiritually united to those stupid and cunning
beings who knew how to do nothing but talk of misery; 96). Out of
necessity to survive, Natividad modifies his attitude, but he is not
convinced that he belongs in Cervelión's dwelling as a replacement
for Cruz María. Subsequently, Natividad maintains his distance,
including his distance from the oral tradition:

> En los cuentos se revelaban los grados de inteligencia y espiri-
> tualidad de aquellos seres. Algunos eran simplísimos elemen-
> tales; otros complicados y llenos de humor. Había narradores es-
> pecializados en relatos espeluznantes, lúgubres y sobrenaturales,
> de aparecidos y brujerías; otros en fábulas alegres e ingeniosas, en
> las que bullía el sentimiento humano del valor y de la astucia

encarnados en los animales del bosque. Las hazañas de Tío Conejo y Tío Tigre resultaban interminables y Venancio el Pajarero
las conocía todas. (84–85)

(In the stories the degree of intelligence and spirituality of those
beings was revealed. Some were simply elemental; others compli-
cated and filled with humor. There were narrators specialized in
hair-raising tales, gloomy and supernatural, of ghosts and witchcraft; others in happy and clever fables, which fermented the human sense of value and boldness embodied in the animals of the
forest. The deeds of Brer Rabbit and Brer Tiger were endless, and
Venancio the Bird Man knew them all.)

As a result of Natividad's inability to penetrate the mythic black
world of Cumboto, the reader is also kept at a distance. The degree
of cultural distance between Natividad and black culture is exemplified most dramatically by the words "those beings" rather than an
identification with a collective "we." There are references to and
brief descriptions of black cultural activities, but they do not come
alive with the forcefulness of situations in *Black St. John's Eve*. The
Brer Rabbit stories told by Venancio are not didactic but rather "ha-
cían reir a los Negros" (made the blacks laugh). His Pedro Grimales
stories are parables of daily life in Cumboto without the strong
Afrocentric undergirding of many Brer Rabbit tales. The conclusion
to be drawn is that there is an awareness of the Afro-Venezuelan
oral tradition in *Cumboto*, but it remains nonfunctional.

Although Roso, whom Abuela Anita does not approve of and
who is the motivating force behind revenge for Cruz María, is portrayed as a negative force in the novel, he is one of a few strong
black figures in *Cumboto*. Abuela Anita shares her misgivings with
Natividad:

Según el juicio de la Abuela, el hermano de Cervelión, que tanto
se parecía a éste en lo físico, era su antípoda en lo normal. También
ella le conoció desde joven y supo de sus andanzas. Había sido un
rebelde, un resentido. Cuando muchacho abandonó la casa de sus
amos en Goaiguaza y fue a alzarse en las montanas del Yaracuy.
Formó con otros una cimarronera. Por aquellos montes cometió
muchas tropelías, asaltó viajeros para robarlos, incluso raptó mu-
jeres blancas. (94–95)

(According to Granny's judgement, Cervelión's brother [Roso],
who looked so much like him physically, was his antithesis under
normal conditions. She also knew him as a youngster and found
out about his deeds. He had been a rebel, a malcontent. When he
was young he abandoned his master's house in Goaiguaza and
took up arms in the mountains of Yaracuy. With others he formed a

maroon movement. In those mountains he committed many atrocities, assaulted travelers to rob them, even violated white women.)

Roso not only fled from the house of his owner but also bashed his
brains out, wreaked havoc in the countryside as a maroon, participated in a civil war, exacted revenge for Cruz María's killing, and
lived to tell war stories about it all. Yet Natividad, who has not
experienced oppression of the same level as Roso, cannot comprehend how a person such as Roso can exist; Natividad remains
the man in the middle, unable to participate fully in either black or
white culture because of a basic ignorance of both.

After Natividad is expelled from the White House, he is forced to
become immersed in Afro-Venezuelan culture, including the myths,
legends, stories, and other manifestations of shared, learned behavior, such as the process of nicknaming: "A Cruz María le llamó el
Matacán, a Prudencio el *Pitirri*, a Pascua la *Culebrita*. A mí desde el
primer momento me bautizó el *Bachaco*" (They called Cruz Maria
"Deer," Prudencio "Kingbird," Pascua "Little Snake." From the first
moment they baptized me "Red"; 85). All of these nicknames are
functional and revealing of the different characters they portray,
especially in the case of Natividad. His role as an unreliable narrator
is reinforced by his physical presentation in the novel as *Bachaco*, a
problematic naming indeed. According to Juan Pablo Sojo: "In the
midst of the dark work force were sprinkled groups of that human
type *catiruano* or *bachaco*, with saffron colored hair and pink skin,
speckled at times with moles; the albinos—whose end result is an
unknown in the mix as white as pillows suspended in a fence."[4]
Natividad, as an albino, appears to be the product of a negative
miscegenation process, as is the case with the children of Fernando
Arguíndegui. A true "unknown," could Natividad be the product
of a black father and a white mother, a product of the womb of doña
Beatriz as he so much wanted to be? Or is Natividad to transcend
the role of a racial abstraction, literary construct, that allows the
author to delve into both black and white modes of existence? What-
ever the answer, it is important to shed light on the fact that Nativi-

4. "Notas para un estudio sobre el regimen esclavista en Venezuela," 264. María
Josefina Tejera's *Diccionario de venezolanismos* offers several definitions of *bachaco*:
"(1) Hormiga grande y voraz de color rojizo y a veces negro de la que se conocen
muchas especies; (2) Hombre listo para buscar el sustento diario; (3) Se aplica al
cabello muy ensortijado y rojizo" ([1] A large and voracious ant of reddish and at
times black color of which many species are known; [2] A man ready to look for his
daily sustenance; [3] It's applied to very curly and reddish hair; 81–82). In the Afro-
Venezuelan context, this term as defined by Juan Pablo Sojo takes on a more profound meaning regarding ethnicity.

dad, the narrator, is not characterized as being completely *negro* but as both a mental and a physical oddity. This is the key to the ethnic ambiguity implicit in the worldview of *Cumboto*.

Underlying the theme of miscegenation in *Cumboto* is the idea of the Afro-Venezuelan oral tradition, kept alive primarily through the stories of Venancio, the Birdman, whom Natividad comes to know after his expulsion from the White House. Venancio's repertoire is composed of episodes that are folkloric, magical, and historical. Aspects of the oral tradition thrive among the vibrant black population, whose situation is described by the narrator as "aquella existencia oscura y reptil de los negros tenía ciertos encantos que yo no hubiese vivido siglos" (that dark and reptile existence of the blacks had certain enchantments that I wouldn't have lived for centuries; 84). As an outsider to the black community, Natividad learns to appreciate Venancio's skill at making relevant both earthly and divine stories. In contrast, five days later Natividad has problems with the episode surrounding witchcraft and the death of don Guillermo. After witnessing the rite of revenge for Cruz María's death and the subsequent demise of don Guillermo, Natividad is perplexed because he is not sure he has witnessed anything and because he does not believe the power of Cervelión and Roso is superior to that of don Guillermo:

> Había "algo" en mí que repugnaba creer en las brujerías de los negros. Todo eso, decíame es una farsa ridícula: los ensalmos, las oraciones, los bojones "preparados." Pero este "algo" sólo influía en una modesta región de mi espíritu; el resto creía, creía sin poder remediarlo, con toda la fuerza que presta el miedo a está clase de sentimentos. Creía, sobre todo, de noche cuando había luna y soplaba el viento mugiendo. (114)

> (There was "something" in me that prohibited me from believing in the witchcraft of blacks. All that, I said to myself, is a ridiculous farce: the incantations, the prayers, the prepared potions. But this "something" only affected a modest region of my spirit; the rest I believed, I believed without being able to remedy it with all the force that lends fear to this class of feelings. I believed, above all, at night when there was a moon and the howling wind blew.)

Since Natividad's presence is ambivalent, it is not surprising that he balks at a black, folk-based ritual that is harmful to the majority culture. Afro-Venezuelan culture is perceived as a phenomenon that is exotic, fantastic, and unreal.

In the chapter "Junio" ("June"), for instance, the fiesta of San Juan, the Feast of St. John the Baptist, serves merely as a backdrop

for the budding romance between Federico and Pascua. The treatment afforded to this most important Afro-Venezuelan holiday in
Cumboto is markedly inferior in both breadth and depth to the interpretations it is given in *Black St. John's Eve*. Rather than being free
expressions of the Afro-Venezuelan soul, events associated with
San Juan are perceived in *Cumboto* as marginal and suspect. Although the celebration of the Feast of Saint John is the most important religiously syncretic ceremony of Afro-Venezuelan culture, its
significance is downplayed. In this particular instance, the official
celebration of the Catholic Church is seen as superior to the popular
manifestation of black culture.

Further underlying the theme of miscegenation in *Cumboto*, where
the author employs Natividad as the bridge between black and
white, is a motif germane to Venezuelan letters—*civilización vs. barbarie* (civilization vs. barbarity)—which is best exemplified by the
Venezuelan writer Rómulo Gallegos. In *Cumboto*, it is the civilized
Europeans, personified in the succession of Arguíndeguis and Lamarcas, who have come to dominate the barbarous black maroon
descendants of Cumboto's environs. The ultimate goal of miscegenation is achieved in the Federico/Pascua relationship, which Natividad views as being complete when their son returns. Following
this line of reasoning, it is difficult to comprehend how Maurice
Belrose arrives at his conclusion that "the list of Venezuelan novels
is long in which the black, the zambo, and the mulatto carry out an
important or fundamental role and where they are given a war-
ranted tribute with *Cumboto* being one of the most beautiful."[5]

Cumboto is hardly a benevolent portrayal of Afro-Venezuelans.
Rather, the message seems to be that the further removed blacks are
from the African somatic norm, the more civilized they are and the
more ready they are for progress in Venezuelan society. The same is
true for black culture as perceived by Natividad, who is unable to
penetrate beyond the folkloric.

Part three of *Cumboto*, "Hágase la luz" ("Let There be Light"),
recounts the four years spent in exile by Natividad away from the
White House. The deadbeat relatives of doña Beatriz, Jer Gunther
Zeus and Laura and Teresa Lamarca, arrive to try and take financial
advantage of the declining economic situation. Federico returns af-
ter five years in Europe and resettles Natividad in his old quarters.
Jer Gunther's daughter, Lotha, arrives with the intent of marrying
Federico, but the plan backfires. In a fit of rage, Federico expels the
Europeans from Cumboto. During the process, Jer Gunther, always

5. *La sociedad venezolana en su novela, 1890–1935*, 118.

looking for Cumboto's alleged buried treasure, assaults doña Beatriz—leaving her paralyzed—and a human skull is found in Beatriz's
closet. It is assumed that this skull belongs to Jaime Rojas, Beatriz's
mulatto piano teacher and lover of decades past.

At this juncture in the novel, Natividad is once again content to
be Federico's shadow. In one of Federico's fits of depression, he tells
Natividad:

> Tú eres para mí algo más que un amigo: juntos nacimos y juntos
> nos levantamos aquí, en Cumboto. Si pudiera pensarse en un
> espíritu de hombre formado por dos naturalezas distintas, yo diría
> que tú y yo formamos ese espíritu. Tú eres como la parte pura de
> la tierra; yo debiera ser su inteligencia. (181)

> (To me you are more than a friend: we were born together and
> together we grew up here, on Cumboto. If I were able to think
> about a spirit of man formed by two different natures, I would say
> that you and I form that spirit. You are like the pure part of the
> earth and I must be its intelligence.)

Although they were born and bred under virtually the same circumstances, Federico assumes that by virtue of his color and European
background he is superior to Natividad. Again, the forces of civilization and barbarity are at work. Natividad concurs with Federico's assumptions because he prefers the ideology of the dominant
class and is consistent in his disdain for black culture. His adverse
reaction to the celebration of the Feast of St. John the Baptist is indicative. From a European perspective, Afro-Venezuelan ceremonies
associated with Saint John the Baptist are barbarous and primitive.
Instead of viewing these phenomena as attempts to create syncretic
forms of worship and celebration, Natividad denigrates these modes
of expressive culture. He demonstrates no sympathy for the "cantos
selváticos" (jungle songs) and the dances with their "fuerza primi-
tiva y elemental" (primitive and elemental force).

Natividad's attitude toward Pascua, Federico's black lover, is also
curious. In spite of her apparent intelligence, talent, and sensuality,
Natividad views Pascua as a lower animal life-form, somewhere
between a bird and a reptile. Due to his own inhibitions, Natividad
cannot understand Federico's obsession with Pascua, an attraction
that is completely physical. Yet out of loyalty to Federico, Natividad
is willing to risk his life in a fight with José del Carmen, Pascua's
betrothed, so that Federico can continue to satisfy his sexual urges.

The fourth part of *Cumboto*, "Frenesí" ("Frenzy"), deals with the
spiraling series of events that leads to the unraveling of the fictions

associated with the rulers of Cumboto. Federico is at the eye of the storm as Pascua leaves him to avoid scandal and Abuela Anita's trunk arrives to fill in the missing gaps in the Lamarcas' and the Arguíndeguis' respective histories. The *intrahistoria* contained in the series of letters in the trunk amounts to an airing of dirty linen in public. Most loose ends are tied up, with the exception of the origins of Natividad.

The episode woven around Anita's trunk is the culminating point of *Cumboto*. There is a return to the present with the appearance of Pascua's son, who has come to inherit Cumboto. He is the product of the miscegenation, the biological synthesis that is also manifest at the cultural level, symbolized by his mastery of both classical and popular music. This dual fusion is what Federico could not achieve.

Abuela Anita is the most important character in *Cumboto* in relation to the historical evolution of the people and their region. She is to history what Venancio is to folklore. Her trunk holds the key to more than a century of Cumboto's complex past. Much of Cumboto's history is contained in letters from members of the Arguíndegui family who officially "founded" and settled Cumboto in the early nineteenth century. In a letter from Matilde Arguíndegui to her brother Carlos dated January 1853 (as they were about to sell Cumboto), Federico reads: "Esta Ana carga todavía el baúl que le entregaste a su abuelo, pero por más que hemos hecho no hemos dado con su paradero" (This Ana still carries the trunk which you sent to your grandfather, but try as we may we have not found its resting place; 206). In the letters, Federico's grandfather Lorenzo Lamarca, who according to Matilde "se dice pariente nuestro y nos extorsiona sin campasión" (says he's our relative and extorts us without compassion; 206), is shown eventually gaining control of Cumboto through deceptive business tactics, and the past hostility between the two clans becomes more clear to Natividad and Federico, who were ignorant of these events.

The trunk, billed as Anita's revenge, is a metaliterary device which allows Natividad to mix reality and fantasy, truth and lie, as he re-creates the *intrahistoria* of Cumboto. As he reads the documents contained in this vessel, Federico receives a shocking view of the private lives of his not-too-noble predecessors on the Arguíndegui side of the family. Most revealing to him is the relationship of his mother with "Jaime Rojas, maestro de escuela y profesor de piano. Moreno, pelo rizado, ojos verdosos, buen mozo" (Jaime Rojas, schoolteacher and piano instructor. Dark skinned, curly haired, greenish eyes, a good looking guy; 208). It is revealed that Beatriz and Jaime were the parents of Cruz María, who upon his birth was taken from the White House and placed at the door of Cervelión so that he would not be killed by Beatriz's father. Jaime was apparently not so fortunate, since the suspicion is that Beatriz guarded his skull in her closet for many years. This intertwining of passions and genes is central to the development of *Cumboto*'s primary thesis regarding miscegenation.

In the worldview of *Cumboto*, miscegenation is espoused as the answer to the ethnic dilemma in Venezuela. Natividad as narrator, protagonist, and witness to both observed and participatory events borrows generously from oral history and the experiences of others to formulate an intertextual collage of ethnic relations in a closed colonial environment. In his analysis of *Cumboto*, Stanley Cyrus writes that

> despite this seemingly positive attitude of Ramón Díaz Sánchez toward Blacks, he simultaneously engages in crude stereotyping, often debases the Afro-Venezuelan folk activities he depicts, and demonstrates a marked disdain for darker skinned Blacks, all of which reflects a Eurocentric mentality and a sharing of some of the hollow racist notions so prevalent in some sectors of the Venezuelan society.[6]

Cyrus's comment reaches to the core of the ironic dimension of *Cumboto* regarding race and class. Since Natividad is the narrator, how does one justify his apparent negative opinion of blackness? Or is he merely a vehicle for the author to espouse deep-seated feelings of color and class or the superiority of the *mulato* to the *negro*?

In her article "Patriarchism and Racism: The Case of *Cumboto*," Rosemary Geisdorfer Feal offers some provocative conclusions regarding ethnic dynamics in the novel:

> In *Cumboto*, therefore, it should not be surprising that the black man seeks out the white woman (and vice versa), be it through a conscious or an instinctual process. Clearly, there is no organized alliance of white women and black men against patriarchal society in the novel, but there is implied rebellion in their forbidden relationships. The races mix but the races clash. However, when it is the privileged white male who fathers a mulatto, quite a different situation evolves. The black mother, Pascua, disappears from Cumboto but her *son* returns to deliver his people into a new era, symbolized by his music. Patriarchal oppression will be prolonged; only man's color has varied.[7]

6. "Ethnic Ambivalence and Afro-Hispanic Novelists," 30.
7. "Patriarchism and Racism," 28.

These remarks are true regarding the ideology of miscegenation expressed in *Cumboto*. There are three mulatto products germane to the novel. Cruz María is the son of Beatriz and Jaime Rojas; both father and son are killed for invading white sexual space at Cumboto. Fernando, Anita's grandson, marries a white European woman and returns to Cumboto only long enough to denigrate the black people. The unnamed son of Federico and Pascua is the new mulatto prototype who symbolically holds the key to Venezuela's ethnic future. These situations reflect the historical sexual reality of Venezuela and much of Spanish America. The white male is *the* legitimate progenitor in the bleaching process. This is part of the colonial legacy of the Americas, which is brought into clearer focus by Manuel Zapata Olivella in a recent publication:

> The scarcity of black women and their high cost determined that for the male slave it was much easier to make it with an indigenous woman than with a companion of his own race. African women, carefully selected by the traffickers for the most strong and beautiful, were immediately hoarded by the white landowners, colonial administrators, creoles and soldiers. . . . As a consequence of this monopoly the miscegenation of mulattos between Spaniards and black women was superior to that of the zambo descendants of the unions between blacks and indigenous people.[8]

Federico acts out a different version of this equation of domination when he attempts to consume and is in turn consumed by the sensuous Pascua. Natividad helps to support this system when he challenges one of her suitors in defense of Federico's aims. The outcome is certain and explicit in the novel's worldview. Miscegenation is acceptable so long as the dominant factor is the white male.

There is a great deal of hatred and self-hate evident in the words and deeds of some black characters in *Cumboto*. Given the novel's implicit sexual hypocrisy, one would expect Frau Berza to publicly put Natividad in his place while maintaining a five-year private relationship with Cruz María. Natividad's reaction to Cruz María's death is that the fault lies in his mixed blood. In Natividad's mind, Cruz María is not being punished solely for what is seen by the narrator as a bold act but also because of his ethnic composition. Subsequently, miscegenation and its consequences address the issue of the archetypal scapegoat at a biological level.

Don Guillermo's attitude regarding blacks is explicit. In an exchange with Federico regarding the discovery of a skull on Cum-

8. *Las claves mágicas de América: Raza, clase y cultura*, 47.

boto, the child asks if it is human, and the father retorts: "—No; la calavera de un negro" (—No; the skull of a black; 58). Don Guillermo's reaction when he finds out that the man he has killed is Cruz María, in contrast to Natividad's reaction to Cruz's death, is that the victim had disrespected his house. As owner of the White House and the land and people attached to it, don Guillermo automatically commands respect, something which he certainly does not merit. The irony of the situation is that he kills his wife's unrecognized son and brother of his own children.

Another dimension of the mulatto dilemma in Cumboto is played out through the figure of Dr. Fernando Arguíndegui, specialist in tropical medicine. Fernando's father was the son of Abuela Anita, who left home with the intent of improving himself and his people: "Habia querido casarse con una blanca por mejorar la raza, 'para emancipar a sus hijos', como decia" (He had wanted to marry a white woman to improve the race, 'to emancipate his children,' as is said; 180). Fernando follows the same route to bleaching as his father, but the results are not as expected:

> Después de haber vivido horas inefables al verse reproducido en dos hijos blancos, de crespos rubios como el lino, su último niño nació negro. Esta era una de las cosas que deseaba contar a la Abuela para consolarla de haber perdido aquel hijo al que nunca olvidaba. Su gran tragedia tenía aspectos cómicos: sus hijos blancos, a medida que iban creciendo, mudaban de color, evolucionaban hacia una palidez sucia y áspera; el cutis tornábaseles opaco como el de una fruta cortada antes de madurar; la cabellera tendía a rizarse y adquiría matices heterogéneos, azafranados, fibrosas, ajabonados . . . (180–81)

> (After having lived ineffable hours upon seeing himself reproduced in two white children with blonde curls like flax, his last child was born black. This was one of the things he wished to tell Granny in order to console her for having lost that son which she never forgot. His great tragedy had comic aspects: his white children, as soon as they began growing, changed color, they evolved toward a dirty and rough paleness; their skin turned opaque on them like a fruit harvested before ripening; their hair commenced to curl and acquired heterogeneous nuances, saffron like, fibrous, dingy . . .)

Fernando's attempt to "better the race" has played a cruel hoax upon him. The "salto para atrás" (leap backward) that his children suffered is the equivalent of divine punishment for his mixed blood. This is the supreme rebuff to pseudobiological engineering and occurs interestingly enough when the mulatto man is progenitor.

Consider that doña Beatriz's and Frau Berza's lovers are killed by white males who are protecting their own false honor and that Fernando's children are presented as abnormal. It is also worthy to mention that the white women Fernando and his father marry are not Venezuelan.

Federico's mulatto son, however, whose arrival frames the narrative of *Cumboto*, is presented in a different light. Natividad is impressed by his biological composition. It is this ethnic synthesis from the dominant culture which unifies and provides a future for the people of Cumboto. The metaphorical music that he plays symbolizes a new dawn, evident in the fact that he is adept in both the classical and popular music traditions, a biological and cultural bridge. The piano, with its black on white keys, ebony and ivory, is a metaphor for this biological synthesis.

Federico, the focus of the novel and current owner of Cumboto, is trapped between two worlds: the black environment of Cumboto and the white European milieu where he was educated and which he prefers. Since Federico cannot abandon Cumboto, he seeks a cultural synthesis through music and sex: "¿Sabes cúal es mi sueño? Amalgamar el alma de está tierra con el espíritu clásico. Hay que crear esa nueva expresión musical y yo la crearé. Ustedes tienen sus cantos, sus ritos, pero no existe sino una música" (You know what my dream is? Amalgamate the soul of this land with the classical spirit. One must create that new musical expression and I shall create it. You all have your songs, your rites, but there does not exist but one music; 212).

Federico's dream is realized in his son. In the powerful last scene of *Cumboto*, the son plays the different movements of Beethoven's sonata *Aurora,* causing a great deal of emotional turmoil among the people of Cumboto, since he interweaves the sonata with elements of Afro-Venezuelan music. The son's version of *Aurora* symbolizes a new beginning in the biological and cultural synthesis of Cumboto. Since the mulatto is skilled in both African and European cultural traditions, it is he who theoretically holds the key to Venezuela's future.

Music is an important thematic and structural motif in *Cumboto*, from the onomatopoeic drum sounds of its Afro-Venezuelan title to the images of European culture projected by the rulers of the plantation. Musicians are involved in most of the novel's basic conflicts involving Europeans. There is an affinity for Beethoven, whose works are alluded to at strategic points throughout the novel. His sonatas *Pathetique* and *Appassionata* are used to illustrate different mental states, especially in the case of Federico.

The *Appassionata*, composed by Beethoven in 1804–1805, serves as a symbolic basis for the intense affair between Federico and Pascua as they share many intimate moments. Perhaps these episodes were designed to mirror the life of Beethoven, since this particular sonata was composed during his "heroic phase" of 1803–1808, a time during which the composer was coming to grips with his deafness and his love for Josephine Von Brunsvik.[9] This composition of great artistic extremes—which range from meditation to exuberation—exacerbates the mood swings of Federico from depression to elation. The use of music to set the tone and capture the mood and environment of characters such as the pathetic Beatriz is also very successful in *Cumboto*.[10]

In his analysis of the relationship between worldview and narrative structure in *Cumboto*, Daniel Piquet writes that "*Cumboto* aspires to re-create the world as the blacks live it, that is to say, the black vision of the world from within. In *Cumboto* the protagonist is the narrator, the one who writes the novel."[11] The metaliterary dimension of *Cumboto* is manifest in the way the history of the plantation is woven together from memories, eyewitness accounts, letters, and other narrative devices. The author's strategy of using Natividad as a cultural spy is skillful and pervasive. By imbuing a black narrator with a white mentality, the dominant ideology regarding class, ethnicity, intelligence, sex, and other cultural factors is allowed to prevail.

The "black worldview from within" that Díaz Sánchez attempts to re-create is different and distant from the interpretations of Afro-Venezuelan life presented in *Black St. John's Eve*. The superiority of Sojo's novel is due to authenticity and specificity. Perhaps this difference can be viewed in the presentation of the funeral rite, an episode common to the two novels. While the black child's wake and burial in *Black St. John's Eve* is treated with ritualistic Afrocentric behavior regarding the Mampulorio and other activities, Cruz María is buried amid a great deal of testifying by members of the community without any attempt to relate this event to traditional Afro-Venezuelan burial practices.

9. According to Joseph Kerman and Alan Tyson, "Beethoven, it is clear, was passionately in love; Josephine, though moved by his devotion and keenly concerned with his happiness, his ideals and his art, retained a certain reserve throughout and rejected any intimacy closer than that of warm friendship." In *The New Grove Dictionary of Music and Musicians*, vol. 2, edited by Stanley Sadie (New York: Macmillan, 1980), 364.

10. The artistic imagery of *Cumboto* receives excellent treatment by Janet J. Hampton in "Music and Dance as Media of Character Analysis and Affirmation of a Black Aesthetic in *Cumboto*," 3–9.

11. *La cultura afrovenezolana en sus escritores contemporáneos*, 43.

Magical realism is an important component of *Cumboto* just as it is in *Black St. John's Eve*. As Luis Leal has written, "In Magical Realism the writer confronts reality and tries to decipher it, to discover what there is of mystery in things in life, in human actions."[12] Since the prime objective of magical realism is the discovery of the mysterious relationship that exists between human beings and their circumstances, the entire black cultural intertext of Cumboto is imbued with the spirit of searching for this relationship, albeit from a distance.

The close relationship of Afro-Venezuelans to nature and their positive perceptions of natural phenomena, for instance, are puzzling to Natividad. *Cumboto* therefore is not in tune with the type of anthropocentric ontology that structures much of the relationship between humans and nature in *Black St. John's Eve*. The possibilities are there, but they are not realized. Given the affinity for other animal forms in the novel, it is not surprising that some of Cumboto's blacks resort to folk-based magical practices to solve the don Guillermo problem.

In spite of the distance between the narrator and the black community, it is apparent that the particular attitude and worldview expressed by the black people of Cumboto is an outgrowth of their African religious heritage and continuing resistance to oppression. The central irony of Cumboto is that it was founded by runaway slaves, who as maroons fought to be free from the shackles of oppression:

> Eran esclavos africanos escapados de los depósitos que los negreros europeas poseían en las Antillas, seres enloquecidos por el terror que preferían desafiar las furias del mar a seguir padeciendo los maltratos de sus civilizados amos. (14)

> (They were African slaves escaped from the holding pens that the European slavers had in the Antilles, beings driven mad by terror, so that they preferred to defy the fury of the sea rather than continue suffering the mistreatment of their civilized owners.)

This traditional defiance, the willingness to defy both natural and human forces for self-determination, manifests itself in figures such as Roso and his followers, who are perceived as aberrations. Their acts are at odds with the docility of Cumboto.

Concern about the plight of blacks on Cumboto is expressed in relation to the marital status of Federico, who is not married and

12. "El realismo mágico en la literatura hispanoamericana," 232–33.

does not seem capable of prolonging his lineage. As the novel points out, "En la Casa Blanca hace falta una señora que garantice la prolongación de la casta del amo" (In the White House a woman is missing who would guarantee the prolongation of the owner's caste; 216). This would mean the end of the plantation and its inhabitants. On the surface, the colonial system has been successful in creating a system of dependency for blacks. Paternalism aside, some individual acts are at odds with the narrator's assertion. A form of self-determination and reliance is demonstrated in the independence of Granny and her family, the entrepreneurship of Cervelión, the resistance to domination by Roso and other black war veterans, and the collective act of liberation committed against don Guillermo. Although Natividad projects the image of a harmonious, deafricanized Cumboto on its way toward miscegenation at the end of the novel, there is internal evidence to suggest that blacks will continue to resist their extinction, biological or otherwise. It has been their history from slavery to the present.

3

Manuel Rodríguez Cárdenas

Tambor:
The Black/White Dialectic

In an article entitled "El tema negro en la literatura venezolana" ("The Black Theme in Venezuelan Literature"), Pedro Lhaya, the author of a book on Juan Pablo Sojo and editor of some of his works, is quick to deny the existence of any literary *negritud* in Venezuela:

> It is not possible to speak of Afro-Venezuelan poetry in Venezuelan literature as one talks about Afro-Cuban or Afro-Haitian poetry. There has not been at any time, although there exists the book *Drum* by Manuel Rodríguez Cárdenas and two poems by Juan Pablo Sojo, native of Curiepe, which must be considered within the "blackish" thing or of "negrism." That of Sojo is an isolated demonstration, loose poems, not published in book form, but whose authenticity in their emphasis places them, more appropriately than others, within the *negrista* current.[1]

Lhaya goes on to state, "In Venezuelan literature, narrative, and poetry, the influence of 'negrism' manifests itself in a superficial and fleeting manner." He concludes:

> A different book, and the only one which might be considered framed within the black theme of Venezuelan poetry, is the book *Drum* by the Yaracuyan poet Manuel Rodríguez Cárdenas, published in 1937, and without a doubt influenced by the blackish movement, a tendency toward which the poet has not gravitated lately, *Drum* seeming like the payoff of a tribute to a literary mode more than a conscious and intentional posture toward "negrism."[2]

1. "El tema negro en la literatura venezolana," 35.
2. Ibid., 37.

If those who have access to the publication outlets deny that there is an Afro-Venezuelan literary voice, what real option does the writer who treats black themes have if he wants to be published and read? Silence and negativity, such as that which surrounded Manuel Rodríguez Cárdenas after the publication of *Drum*, are obvious responses. For almost forty years he did not discuss his crucial work, *Drum*. But when the second edition was issued in 1972, Rodríguez Cárdenas had some harsh words for his critics. In his emotional introduction to the book, entitled "A Treinta y Cuatro Años de *Tambor*" ("Thirty-Four Years from *Drum*"), the author remarks:

> Hombre confrontado como he sido siempre y en buena parte por los intelectuales de filigrana, no sé si me aceptaran ahora, cuando ningún peligro implico para ellos que asome la punta de algunas verdades. Pocos libros han producido un impacto tan intenso y generado una onda emocional expansiva como *Tambor*.[3]

> (A confronted man as I have always been and for the most part by paper intellectuals, I don't know if they would accept me now when I pose no threat to them who appear at the edge of some truths. Few books have produced such an intense impact and generated an expansive emotional wave like *Drum*.)

Rodríguez Cárdenas probably had in mind the type of reaction that appeared in *El Heraldo* in 1938, where the anonymous C.M.C.C. wrote at the time: "In Rodríguez Cárdenas the word is not black: the word is white although it refers to blacks. In the poets Guillén, Ballagas, etc., the word and the background are black, with all the qualities and defects of the race."[4] It is indeed ironic that this re-

---

3. *Tambor: Poemas para negros y mulatos*, iii. Unless otherwise noted, further citations are to the second (1972) edition and will be made parenthetically in the text.
4. "Ensayo: Averiguación del mulato en *Tambor*." *Drum* was published at a period when there was a great deal of tension regarding the role of blacks in Venezuela. On the one hand there was the push by white politicians to "blanquear" (lighten) the population, while on the other hand those of mixed origins pressured for power. The Acción Democrática (AD) party, which originated in the 1930s, was the vehicle for the masses to combat discrimination and to change the basic social and economic fabric of Venezuela. In his chapter devoted to "Race and National Image in the Era of Popular Politics, 1935–1958," Winthrop R. Wright observes:

> At one point or another in their lives, most AD leaders felt the sting of racial discrimination in some form. These individuals comprised a diverse lot of men and women of mixed racial origin: Rómulo Betancourt from the state of Miranda, a self-described *café con leche* politician of middle class origin; the mulatto educator, Luis Beltrán Prieto Figueroa from the island of Margarita; Andres Eloy Blanco, a *pardo* poet from Cumara; and Manuel Rodríguez Cárdenas, a light-skinned mulatto writer from the state of Yaracuy. These individuals came to power in the mid–1940's as outsiders. Born and raised outside of Ca-

viewer would attribute more of the characteristics of *negritud* to the works of *negrista* writers such as Emilio Ballagas, Luis Llorens Torres, and Luis Pales Matos than to those of Manuel Rodríguez Cárdenas. This is due, in my opinion, to both a fundamental misunderstanding of what Rodríguez Cárdenas's work represents and to the tendency to deny that there is *Afro* authenticity in Venezuela.

Although Rodríguez Cárdenas displayed the proper protocol and maintained a great deal of social distance between himself and the poetry by not identifying himself too closely with the blacks who populate the volume, there was an adverse response to *Drum*. In the critical comments published in this era, there was ambivalence, but the negative sentiments prevailed. The reaction of R. Olivares Figueroa was typical:

> It corresponds to Manuel Rodríguez Cárdenas the honor of being the first among us to have created a native poetry, inspired in the black soul. It's up to him, in our judgement, to rid himself of outside interests, of the Afro-Antillian, which is super-imposed, of the foolishness and exaggerations. Manuel Rodríguez Cárdenas, who has demonstrated an exceptional disposition for true poetry, must, in our judgement, denouncing impassioned suggestions, delve in his own area—earth and spirit—in order to obtain the elements of creation which can make him, in the long run, the most popular of our poets.[5]

On the one hand Rodríguez Cárdenas is given credit for introducing *negrista* poetry to Venezuela, while on the other hand he is chastised for initiating the Afro-Antillian mode and his authenticity is questioned. From Olivares's perspective, Rodríguez Cárdenas is superimposing alien poetic norms upon Venezuelan circumstances. Following this line of reasoning, to interpret the situation of blacks in verse is not "true" poetry; rather, it has to be nonsense and exaggeration because black culture in Venezuela is not a separate entity. There is an implicit warning in this quote: Rodríguez Cárdenas should forget this *negrista* nonsense if he wishes to be successful as a writer in Venezuela. Rodríguez Cárdenas apparently heeded this advice and never published another major volume of poetry. This critical reaction is typical of those few that have appeared regarding *Drum*. The book was greeted either with negativity, silence, or the implied question, How dare the author pen such a volume?

Drum was, and still is, a controversial book due to the position it

racas, from middle-class families, they attended public rather than private schools and universities, and shared a nonwhite racial origin. (*Café con leche: Race, Class, and National Image in Venezuela*, 99)

5. *Nuevos poetas venezolanos: Notas críticas*, 33.

occupies in Venezuelan cultural history. It predates *Black St. John's Eve* and is a key text in analyzing the development of literary *negritud* and the creation of a minority discourse in Venezuela, an issue which has not been fully explored.

In his introduction to the first (1938) edition of *Drum*, Julian Padron observes that "*Drum* also has a chronological value which is of importance: it is the first quality Venezuelan book on black themes" (xiv). For four decades, *Drum* remained the key work of Venezuelan poetry expressing black themes. *Drum* contains a variety of selections, but primary emphasis is placed upon the Afro-Venezuelan experience, as the collection's subtitle suggests. Although Rodríguez Cárdenas treated the correct topics with some of the proper sounds and rhythms, he was not able to capture the essence of *lo negro*. Dance, music, and other ritualistic activities populate Rodríguez Cárdenas's *negro* and *mulato* poetry, but they do not diminish the apparent cultural distance between poet and material. Rodríguez Cárdenas's poetry, just as the landmark essay by Díaz Sánchez, builds upon the biblical image of Ham and the theme of the black as a pariah. In fact, the title of the first poem in the volume is "El manifiesto de Cam" ("Ham's Manifesto").

The first edition of *Drum* contains twenty-seven poems and is divided into five sections: "Socotora" (eight poems); "Frente al Cabo Guardafuí" ("Facing Cape Guardafui," six poems); "Grito Mulato" ("Mulatto Shout," eight poems); "Banderas" ("Flags," four poems); and the single poem "La Gesta de Faustino Parra" ("The Deed of Faustino Parra"). These selections are focused primarily upon the Afro-Venezuelan cultural intertext. The second edition is a reprint with the introductory remarks by Manuel Rodríguez Cárdenas cited above.

"Socotora" contains the poems "Ham's Manifesto," "Tamunango," "Tu risa" ("Your Smile"), "Habladurías" ("Ramblings"), "El merengue final" ("The Last Merengue"), "Negro viejo" ("Old Black Man"), "Canción de la Negra Juana" ("Black Juana's Song"), and "Apuntes para un close-up de Eusebia Cosme" ("Notes for a Close-up of Eusebia Cosme").

"Ham's Manifesto" takes as its point of departure the so-called biblical condemnation of Ham and his people due to disobedience to God, the account of which appears in Genesis. As the darker elements of the human race, the Hamites are condemned to perpetual suffering and discrimination. This poem lends a sympathetic ear to the plight of this group of people, and it encourages blacks to overcome and assert themselves. The initial series of images, however, is nonpositive and degrading in a physical sense:

Negro campañero,
de manos de zarpa y ojos de alacrán;
negro encadenado
de rotas rodillas y gestos de cal
negro sin bitácora
perdido en la tela de araña
de la sociedad.

(1)

(Black companion
with clawlike hands and scorpion eyes;
chained black
with broken knees and faces of lime
black man without direction
lost in the spider web
of society.)

The lesser-animals metaphor functions to exacerbate the situation of blacks, who are not only prisoners of society but also uncertain entities in the human/nonhuman animal order of things. Clawlike hands and scorpion eyes are features brought into clear focus by society's spider web, which stifles blacks. The blacks are chained, homeless, and worked to the brink of oblivion in an uncaring society.

Within its nonpositive beginning, the poem takes a historical focus: the lines "Negro berebere, cabila o tuaregue / venido de un mundo que ya se olvidó" (Black Berber, Cabinda or Tuaregue / you came from a world you have forgotten) conjure up rhetorical images of Africa. However, the negative air surrounding black existence persists, reaching its culminating point in the fifth stanza:

Negro despreciable sin Ras Mulagueta
que te abre al machete los reinos de Dios;
negro sin paraguas, sin colcha ni abrigo;
negro sin amigos, negro sin poetas
hoy estamos solos tu tristeza y yo

(3)

(Despicable black without Ras Malagueta
who opens to you the kingdom of God with his machete;
black man without an umbrella, without a pillow or overcoat;
black man without friends, black man without poets
today we are alone your sadness and I)

The dispossessed black who enters heaven only through force, stripped of material and spiritual comforts, is offered solidarity with the poetic "I": "Aquí están mis nervios, aquí están mis fuerzas, y aquí están mis versos para tu bongó" (Here are my nerves, here are my strengths, and here are my verses for your bongo). The final call, to "Wake up now black man / Extend your arms / Let's march to the beat of your proud tam-tam," is made within an environment of qualified support for black affirmation. Throughout this poem, blacks are presented as a poor people, deprived of culture and will, who need a special incentive to assert themselves. Image clusters are effective in further dehumanizing them.

The final verses of "Ham's Manifesto" are "radical" to the extent that they call for positive acts on the part of blacks to transform themselves from the role of victims to the role of protagonists in the society:

> Que se hunda en el polvo la frente del mundo!
> Nada nos importe, negro tremebundo.
> Destruyamos esto para que resurjan
> sobre un campo nuevo tus patas de araña,
> tus flores, tus cantos, tus frágiles cañas,
> tu triste derecho de un trozo de pan.
>
> (5)
>
> (Let the face of the world sink in the dust!
> Nothing matters to us, dreadful black man.
> Let's destroy that so there will reappear
> upon a new ground your spider feet,
> your flowers, your songs; your fragile bones,
> your sad right to a crust of bread.)

The message of "Ham's Manifesto" is that because blacks have been shackled with stereotypes based upon Christian myths, they have had to combat false assumptions and resist being condemned to the lower echelon of society.

The poem "Tamunango," which borrows its title from the name of a popular dance, treats an aspect of Afro-Venezuelan popular culture. The multifaceted dimensions of the dance are captured in the poem's portrayal of its sights, sounds, and smells. The *mina* drum sets the tone and rhythm of the event, which takes special meaning as it tries to link the African diaspora: "Nervios que se tuercen entre el telegrama / que manda la raza desde el Tombuctú" (Nerves that twist around the telegram / the race sends from Timbuktu; 7). Blackness is the metaphor that dominates the scene: "Es el negro aceite de la raza negra que empieza a chorrear" (It's the black oil of the black race which begins to flow). This basic image of

black sweat is amplified in subsequent stanzas by allusions to "petroleum," "black whip," "carbon," and "coal colored." The black
woman plays a traditional rhythmic role: "Menía la cintura. Sacá
bien lo pechos. Dale despacito . . ." (She wiggled her waist, thrust
her breasts out. Does it slowly . . .); she is described as "—Cuerpito
e culebra" (—Body of a snake; 9). The atmosphere is one of joyous
celebration:

> Y los negros bailan. Se estiran, se encogen,
> ondulan, se mueven, se encharcan en barro del fétido olor.
> Las negras titilan con el sexo al aire
> surcado de venas y hediondo a sudor.
>
> (11)
>
> (And the blacks dance. They expand, retract,
> wave, move, wallow in the mud with the repugnant smell.
> The black women quiver with their sex in the open air
> furrowed with veins and stinking of sweat.)

This particular image of the dancers is nonpositive; they are portrayed as a foul, stinky mass of humanity. Moreover, the party is
disrupted by the authorities because one of the participants, a boot-
black, is caught with, ironically, a "caja vacía de Shinola" (empty
can of Shinola) that apparently has been stolen but which he needs
to practice his profession. The poem ends on a dark note as the
night reigns: "y el río silencioso copia las cabezas / de los negros
que huyen por el callejón" (and the silent river captures the heads /
of the blacks as they flee through the alley; 11).

"Your Smile" also builds on the metaphor of blackness exemplified in the person of a black woman:

> Si te escondieras de noche
> se asustaría la neblina
> porque eres, negra, tan negra,
> que en tu pizarrón de carne
> la noche se vuelve tiza.
>
> (15)
>
> (If the night could hide you
> the fog would be frightened
> because you are, black, so black,
> that in your blackboard of flesh
> the night becomes chalk.)

The poem is a projection of positive sentiment upon this figure who
exemplifies and embodies inherent characteristics of her people.

"Ramblings" conjures up images of a promised land for blacks, a land of milk and honey where there are no worries. The technique of call and response is employed, with each positive pronouncement followed by "¡Bamonó pa allá!" (Let's go over there!). "Ramblings" is an exercise in verbal frustration:

—Esa tierra, trigueños,
Yo lo sabía.
Pero . . . perdí los libros
de geografía
Negro que nace negro,
negro se va
y estas cositas güenas
que yo he pintao
son puras invenciones
pa conversá!
(21)

(—That land, brown ones,
Was known to me.
But . . . I lost the books
of geography
A black who is born black,
remains black
and these good things
that I have pictured
are pure inventions
for talking!)

This poem is written in the popular dialect of the region, with the intent of capturing patterns of its speech and distinguishing it from the official linguistic registers. The ironic conclusion of the poem is that even in their fantasies, blacks are denied the possibility of transcending the all-important factor of color.

"The Last Merengue" is a tribute to the rhythm and body of Rosedá, a black dancer: "El cuerpito retinto se tuerce y salta / se acurruca, se curva, se parte en dos" (The blue black body twists and jumps / screws, curves, breaks in two; 25). Rosedá is a hip-swaying, butt-shaking presence who complements the musical expression of the drum.

"Old Black Man" implores an individual at the end of his life cycle to continue resisting the humiliation imposed upon him by the white world. In an insensitive and uncaring universe, he is encouraged not to give up in this world and to "echa como una tropa pululante y babosa / tus gusanos calientes sobre la humanidad" (spew like a swarming and slimy troop / your hot worms upon society; 21) from the grave. He is instructed not to leave this world without a meaningful trace.

"Black Juana's Song" is the most developed, in a literary sense, of the sensuous portrayals of female dancers in the poetry of Manuel Rodríguez Cárdenas. As he sets the scene for the carnival at which Juana will perform, the poet laments:

> pero yo, el poeta triste,
> sólo le canto a la negra,
> porque Juanita es el alma-
> mater de mi barrio abstracto:
> síntesis de los abuelos
> de toda la vecindad
>
> (33)

> (but I, the sad poet,
> sing only to the black woman,
> because Juana is the alma
> mater of my abstract barrio:
> synthesis of the grandparents
> of the whole neighborhood)

Just as this barrio is imagined, so is the larger-than-life Juana a figment of the poet's imagination. She raises the art of dance to another level in terms of its complexity and performance:

> La negra baila un merengue
> y a más de bailar, parece
> que se está deshilachando
> sobre su cuerpo un torrente
> de adormecida lascivia
>
> (37)

> (The black woman dances a merengue
> and more than dancing, it seems
> that there is unraveling
> upon her body a torrent
> of calm lasciviousness)

In spite of her physical prowess and dancing accomplishments, Juana apparently has a problem. The narrator informs the reader that she believes that

> en la vida sin amores
> que la espera, porque es negra

y las negras no conocen
ni novios ni matrimonios.
—Ah malhaya, quién pudiera
ser blanca como la luna!

(26)

(in the life without loves
that awaits her, because she is black
and black women don't know
either fiancés or marriages.
—Oh damn, if one could
be white like the moon!)

Juana is filled with self-hate because of her blackness; she is a "pain of the race" who longs to be white. She dies three days later—some say because of the black burden, others say because of pneumonia. It seems incongruous that this proud, black presence would be hung up on the problem of color, but this appears to be her fate. Again, irony is a key element in the evolution of Juana as a protagonist.

"Notes for a Close-up of Eusebia Cosme" is a salute to a woman of African descent. The poem makes reference to Afro-Venezuelan commonplaces, and it closes out the first section of *Drum*. From the readings of these nine poems, it is possible to arrive at tentative conclusions regarding Rodríguez Cárdenas's attitude toward blacks. Instead of extolling the positive virtues of blackness, the images and metaphors of which dominate this group of poems, color is viewed by the poet as a burden that inhibits progress and causes low self-esteem among Afro-Venezuelans. Even within the closed environment of their culture, blacks are presented as not using their pride as a positive force to help them confront white society.

Just as other *negrista* poets, such as Pales Matos (with whom he is often compared), Rodríguez Cárdenas demonstrates in this section of *Drum* that he is more descriptive than social, more *costumbrista* (folksy) than lyrical. His attitude is fittingly objective and often ironic. There is no identification by the poet with the culture he describes. He does not appear to be able to go beyond the surface to capture the deep sentiments of Afro-Venezuelans. Rodríguez Cárdenas therefore remains on the outside, immersed in Afro-Venezuelan geography and folklore, with the specter of racism constantly in the background. The poet's inability or hesitancy to capture the essence of black culture in verse leaves the impression that he is ambivalent regarding questions of ethnicity.

"Facing Cape Guardafui," the second section of *Drum*, contains six poems: "La canción de la negrita" ("Song of the Black Girl"),

"Cocuy, Cocuy Batatero," "Consigna para el estudiante negro" ("Assignment for the Black Student"), "La semilla en el surco" ("The Seed in the Furrow"), "Canción de cuna" ("Cradle Song"), and "Infierno del prisionero" ("Prisoner's Hell"). This section shares many of the thematic concerns of the first section in that it continues to explore the black experience.

In "Song of the Black Girl," Consuelo Ruiz is the object addressed by the poet:

> Tú eres negra jabequera,
> caliente como el anís;
> eres parche, río, bandera,
> grito de sol somalí,
> rica nave costanera
> que naufragó en la frontera
> frente al Cabo Guardafui
> (51)

> (You are branded black woman,
> warm as anise;
> You are drum, river, flag,
> a shout of Somali sun,
> a rich costal ship
> which crashed on the border
> facing Cape Guardafui)

Again, the poet concentrates on the external physical qualities of his female protagonist with allusions to a distant, exotic Africa. She is likened to vital elements, politics, and national concerns. The result is an inability to transcend Africa as rhetorical *nomen*, in spite of the analogy between the woman and the archetypal vessel, which in this case is destroyed.

"Cocuy, Cocuy Batatero" is a poem dealing with the folklore of the Yaracuy region, while "Assignment for the Black Student" treats the black experience of struggle and suffering throughout the centuries with an important focus upon education:

> Tú no viniste: Estabas.
> Aquí en la médula,
> Como un callado corazón despierto.
> Y cuando, manos y pies atados, te trajeron,
> en la sentina de los barcos,
> bajo las frías constelaciones
> que retuestan la piel como un sol con insomnio
> y entre los mismos vientos

íbamos apersogados
Somos una misma emoción
y un solo aprendizaje.
                    (61)

(You didn't come: You were.
Here in the marrow,
Like a silent awake heart.
And when, hand and feet tied, they brought you,
in the bowel of the ships,
under the cold constellations
that retoasted the skin like a sun with insomnia
and among the same winds
we went tethered
We are a same emotion
and an only apprenticeship.)

There is identification on a human level between narrator and protagonist. The international gene pool provides the basis for their
mutual experience as persons. Thus, metaphorically, they can be
portrayed as one, emotionally and intellectually. This is truly at the
level of the abstract since the reality is that

El blanco va a la universidad,
el negro va a los campos.
El blanco aprende a leer y escribir
el negro a manejar el hacha.
                    (63)

(The white person goes to the university,
the black person goes to the fields.
The white learns to read and write
the black how to handle an axe.)

The poem is a litany of the pain and suffering experienced by black
people. In the final analysis, the burden with which the black is
faced cannot be resolved by intellectual activity, but by social action.
The fact that this situation has existed since slavery does not bode
well for the future. In this emotionally charged poem, the poet utilizes historical memory to highlight discrimination in the present
through overt identification with the plight of blacks.

"The Seed in the Furrow" recounts the metaphorical sexual union
of two black youngsters, while "Cradle Song" projects a positive
image of a black child at birth, unaware of the harsh realities await-

ing him in the outside world which frames the scene. "Prisoner's Hell" deals with the sexual fantasies of an incarcerated man.

These first two sections of *Drum* are components of an eclectic work which confirms Manuel Rodríguez Cárdenas's status as the initiator of black themes in the national Afro-Venezuelan literary tradition. Stereotypes notwithstanding, there is an awareness by the author, in the second section, of the historical plight of blacks in Venezuela. He pays proper respect to black women, dance, and other aspects of popular culture. He also demonstrates some knowledge of the experience of Afro-Venezuelans, albeit from the surface. Therefore, Manuel Rodríguez Cárdenas goes one step further than the *negrista* poets in his efforts to capture the essence of *lo negro*. The basic problem with these poems is their central ironic thread, which creates a dialectical tension. On the one hand the poet wishes to make blacks the subject of his poetry; on the other hand he does not grant them their total share of humanity.

"Mulatto Shout," the third section of *Drum,* consists of eight poems: "Ay Luis Alberto Domínguez," a lament dedicated to a popular song legend that concerns his death; "Sor Inocencia" ("Sister Innocence"), a religious tribute to a nun; "Así te estoy queriendo" ("This Is How I'm Loving You"), a brief, intense love poem; "Poema en tres cantos del sexo, la raza y la civilización" ("Poem in Three Cantos of Sex, Race, and Civilization"), dedicated to Alicia; "Canción de un hombre a caballo" ("Song of a Horse Rider"), a recognition of a skilled rider; "Silene Luna," an ode to an ephemeral muse; "La plegaria del coplero" ("The Poet's Prayer"), a lament over lost love; and "Tarde de toros coleados" ("Eve of the Bullfight"), which places the inaugural bullfight parade in a positive light.

In this section, there are surface references to the color brown (*moreno*) as the title suggests, but the selection of most depth is "Poem in Three Cantos of Sex, Race, and Civilization." It is divided into three segments, and the poetic convention of apostrophe is used to address "Alicia." The section "Sex" begins:

> Alicia: porque tienes los senos como lomas de oro,
> Olorosos a pulpa de mereyes maduros;
> porque ignora tu sexo la propiedad privada,
> y es tu cuerpo un poema de exaltación marxista.
>   (93)

> (Alicia: because you have breasts like hills of gold,
> Smelly like the pulp of ripe cashews;
> because your sex ignores private property,
> and your body is a poem of marxist exaltation.)

The poem's initial tone is ironic, exemplifying jealousy on the part of the narrator who, displeased that he is not the sole possessor of Alicia's sensuous body, resorts to sociological concepts to get his point across. He equates the sex act with the poetic process:

> —tú te entregas, yo canto;
> tú amarras el molino de tu sexo a otro sexo
> mientras yo me transnocho por hilar dos palabras.
>   (95)

> (—you give of yourself, I sing;
> you tie the grinder of your sex to another sex
> while I spend the night stringing together two words.)

Sex and poetry, it seems, are inextricably bound from the poet's point of view, since both have creative potential.

"Sex" logically leads to the question of "Race," the focus of the second canto:

> El mal está en la sangre, seguramente. En esa
> sangre que nos metieron nuestros antepasados
> entre las curvas venas,
> porque tú tienes mucho de Isabel La Católica
> cuando me das la joya cárdena del pezón
> por verme ser Colón
> del Nuevo Mundo, intacto, de todas tus cosquillas;
> y bastante de aquella margarita de ébano
> que fue Guiomar, la negra rebelde y anacrónica.
>
> Y yo—¿por qué negarlo?—lo mismo podría ser
> un piache macilento de Alejandro Colina,
> que un negro de Hotentocia,
> o Rui Díaz de Bivar.
>
> No somos por lo tanto responsables, Alicia:
> culpa fue de tu abuelo el obispo español,
> de mi tatarabuela (que fue monja descalza)
> y de Fray Bartolomé de Las Casas, el fraile
> que todas las mañanas bendicen mis indígenas
> y cada noche insultan los negros de mi sangre.
>   (96–97)

> (The evil is in the blood, surely. In that
> blood which our ancestors put in us
> between the curved veins,
> because you have a lot of Isabelle the Catholic

when you give me the crown jewel of your nipple
by seeing me as Columbus
of the New World, intact, with all your ticklishness;
and enough of that black pearl
who was Guiomar, the rebellious and anachronistic black.

And I—why deny it?—the same might be
a gaunt resemblance of Alejandro Colina,
as a black Hotentot,
or Rui Díaz de Bivar.

We are not therefore responsible, Alicia:
at fault was your grandfather the Spanish bishop,
and my great grandmother (who was a barefooted nun)
and of Bartolomé de las Casas, the priest
who every morning blesses my indigenous people
and each night insults the blacks of my blood.)

"Race" conjures up images of miscegenation that have been prevalent throughout much of Spanish civilization, a fusion of Christian
(Isabel La Católica), Jewish (Colón), and Moorish/African (Guiomar)
cultures and blood.[6] The basic theme of this segment is the impor-

6. In his book *Entonces el pueblo era pequeño* (*Then the Town Was Small*), Manuel
Rodríguez Cárdenas includes "Los Tambores de Miguel," a fictionalized version of
episodes in the lives of Miguel and Guiomar. Maroonage is the theme of "Los Tambores de Miguel," which has an extraordinary beginning because the narrator serves
as historical witness during the reign of this important prisoner from Africa who
sought to change a portion of Venezuelan history: ". . . que yo anduve con él; que
una tarde nos sentamos—él, Guiomar y yo—en algún rincón del Páramo de Cabim-
bu a matar un gallo negro para una brujería" (. . . that I walked with him; that one
evening we sat down—he, Guiomar, and I—in some corner on the Plain of Cabim-
bu to kill a black rooster for witchcraft; p. 183). Witchcraft and the power of African
culture are factors which sustain Guiomar and Miguel, from the Coast of Guinea, in
their fight to throw off the shackles of bondage imposed by the likes of Juan de
Villegas in 1551. The story ends in a scene of violence as Miguel and his followers
destroy the oppressor. This image of the Venezuelan maroon as unbowing and un-
conquered is in keeping with the accepted assumption that blacks resisted slavery,
passively and actively, to assure their freedom. Again, Manuel Rodríguez Cárdenas
resorts to the Afro-Venezuelan cultural intertext to buttress his fiction.

It is important to mention here that Guiomar was the companion of El Negro
Miguel, one of the most significant Venezuelan maroons, whose rebellious activities
had a far-reaching impact. Miguel Acosta Saignes writes in *Vida de los esclavos negros
en Venezuela*:

El alzamiento del negro Miguel a mediados del siglo XVI, tuvo como resultado
la rebelión de los JIRAJARAS, quienes durante setenta y cinco años fueron irre-
ductibles, y otros hechos como el que mucho después comentaba Humboldt
sobre la república de zambos y mulatos. (259)

(The uprising of black Miguel around the middle of the sixteenth century resulted in the rebellion of the Jirajaras indians, who for seventy-five years were
indomitable, and other events such as those about the republic of *zambos* and
mulattoes which Humboldt commented upon.)

tance of the international gene pool in a society that has always been overly concerned with pureness of blood. This ironic approach to the relationships linking Spanish America to African and European civilizations is an attempt to demystify Spanish icons and relate them to contemporary reality. More importantly, Spanish Americans are perceived as biological amalgams, products of an ongoing genetic exchange.

"Poem in Three Cantos" idealistically projects the protagonist's dreams and aspirations of life with Alicia into the future. This idyllic civilization will be constructed upon the physical presence of Alicia and will encompass both myth and reality. Alongside "a sensual Coney Island" and "a child's ribbon from Mickey Mouse" are allusions to "Apolo" and "Olimpio." Symbolically, Alicia represents Mother Earth: "Luego sobre tus muslos abriremos caminos / y trotaran cien potros de agua por tus venas" (Then between your thighs we will open paths / and a hundred water ponies will gallop through your veins; 53). She also becomes the protectorate of a jealous deity: "Queda un lugar vacío: la gruta de tu sexo / Bajo pena de muerte, ningún mortal podrá / poner su vista en él" (There remains an empty place: the cave of your sex / Under the death penalty, no mortal shall be able / to gaze upon it; 101). The ironic contrast implicit in the poem is the affirmation of sexuality in the creation of civilization and its subsequent denial at the very end. "Poem in Three Cantos" is a dialectical assessment of fundamental issues affecting humankind, and it is one of the best published by Manuel Rodríguez Cárdenas. It explores the mythological as well as the more immediate human aspects of culture.

"Flags," the next section of *Drum*, contains four poems: "A la muerte de Federico García Lorca" ("The Death of Federico García Lorca"), a poignant lament and homage to Rodríguez Cárdenas's Spanish counterpart; "Tántalo" ("Tantalus"), which praises the mythic character and his suffering by relating it to daily experiences; "Manifiesto a una casa" ("A House Manifesto"), which pays tribute to the archetypal abode; and "La escuela rural" ("The Rural School"), which reminisces on grade-school experiences with ex-companions.

Finally, "The Deed of Faustino Parra," the final section of *Drum*, is a mini-epic poem devoted to the character Faustino Parra and his activities. It is divided into four cantos: "Perfil" ("Profile"), "El encuentro" ("Encounter"), "El bandolero" ("Bandit"), and "La muerte" ("Death"). Faustino's life story is played out against a backdrop of discrimination and violence. The protagonist is a social bandit who is initially engulfed in an environment of blackness:

Negro el pelo, negro el rostro,
negro el caballo trotón;
negro el bigote retinto,
negra la mala intención
                    (151)

(Black the hair, black the countenance
black the trotting horse
black the jet-black moustache
black the evil intention)

Like most popular heroes, there is a reason for Faustino's bad intentions. In "Encounter" the poet reveals that

Había visto arder su rancho
como un manojo de esparto
sólo porque entre el cobijo
su vida y su fe tenía
                    (159)

(He had seen his house burn
like a handful of grass
only because in the shelter
he had his life and his faith)

Faustino, it seems, is the victim of an injustice perpetrated against him, not because of some act but because of who he is. He therefore seeks vindication outside of the "law," as other popular heroes (such as Demetrio Macías of Mariano Azuela's *The Underdogs*) do. In "Bandit" Faustino gathers a following and grows in stature as he exacts his revenge: "Faustino iba entre sus hombres / gigantesco, como un Dios" (Faustino went among his men / gigantic, like a god).

"Death" recounts the end of a brave and violent individual who asked no quarter and gave none:

Así terminó Faustino
el de la mala intención;
el que por vengar la pena
de tener la color negra,
sobre el frío de los caminos
muerte y romance sembró
y al que sólo le faltaba
para su consagración
¡el cantor que lo cantara
como lo he cantado yo!
                    (171)

(Thus ended Faustino
he of the evil intention;
he who to avenge the pain
of having a black skin,
upon the chilliness of the roads
sowed death and romance
and he who only lacks
for his consecration
the singer who would sing to him
as to him I have sung!)

There is the same type of ambivalence toward Faustino Parra as has been demonstrated toward the black experience throughout *Drum.* On the one hand the reader is led to believe that Faustino rebels because an atrocity has been committed against him and his family; on the other hand it is stated that Faustino seeks vengeance because he is black. The relationship between blackness and rebellion is developed throughout the poem: "Entonces aquella sangre / hija de sangre africana / que fue nave capitana / de una absurda rebelión" (Then that blood / daughter of African blood / which was flagship / of an absurd rebellion; 170–71). Observations such as these, regarding the "absurdity" of Faustino's acts, keep Manuel Rodríguez Cárdenas at a distance from black culture and keep him from making the bold leap into the poetry of *negritud* in Venezuela. Given the circumstances presented in the poem, Faustino Parra is certainly justified in defending himself and exacting revenge for crimes against him.

In Rodríguez Cárdenas's book *Entonces el pueblo era pequeño* (*Then the Town Was Small*), the fictionalized, prose version of this mini-epic about Faustino Parra fleshes out the poem and deepens the discrepancies between the two versions, contributing to the gaps between fantasy and reality, truth and lie, that are at the basis of most popular legends. The story "Faustino Parra" commences with the cold-blooded murder of an unknown coach driver by Faustino and ends with his own death. Thus the tale is framed within a cycle of violence and destruction. The narrator re-creates the life of Faustino through a series of personal reflections and official documents: "Aquí tengo ante mí, unos papeles viejos. Son expedientes levantados en jurisdicción de Cocorote los años 1891 y 1892 cuando Faustino no era todavía el caballero de la muerte" (Here I have before me, some old papers. They are documents filed in Cocorote in 1891 and 1892 when Faustino was not yet the gentleman of death).[7] Through

7. *Entonces el pueblo era pequeño,* 209. Further references will be made parenthetically in the text.

a combination of popular and official discourse, a portrait of Faustino as a deranged killer emerges.

As in "The Deed of Faustino Parra," the motivation for Faustino's initial violence in the prose work is apparently the destruction of his household:

> La tradición no está descaminada al presumir que Faustino se lanzó a la carrera de la muerte por una mujer, su concubina o su hermana, a la que violentaron unos hombres en el desamparo de su rancho. El negro vio desde lejos la humareda de la candela y apretó el paso, cerro arriba. Cuando llegó al plan ya no quedaba nada de la choza de paja. A un lado echada, como perro medio desnudo, gimoteaba la mujer. . . . La mutiló de un machetazo, para que se acabara de perder todo de una vez. Y se fue cerro abajo. (8)

> (The tradition is not misleading by assuming that Faustino took to the trail of death for a woman, his concubine or sister, who was violated by some men who destroyed his home. The black man saw from afar the smoke of the flame and quickened his step, up the hill. When he arrived at the top nothing remained of the straw hut. Thrown to the side like a half-naked dog, the woman was whimpering. . . . He finished her off with a machete blow so that he could lose all of it at once. And he went back down the hill.)

Negative manifestations of machismo—guns, knives, violence, and false honor—dominate Faustino's life and ultimately lead to his death at the hands of authorities. The poetic version, although not positive, is much more sympathetic than the prose characterization, which is very indeterminate in its presentation of character and circumstances.

In conclusion, Manuel Rodríguez Cárdenas manipulates Afro-Venezuelan themes very well, and in so doing he demonstrates a familiarity with the sights and sounds associated with black culture. His work is a clear example of the difference between black thematics and a black worldview, a demonstration of which is the basic focus of this study. It is necessary to have more than a surface knowledge of black culture in order to imbue works with an Afrocentric vision, a phenomenon which comes from within rather than from without. The discourse of Manuel Rodríguez Cárdenas is replete with images of poetic *negrism*. There are numerous exotic-sounding words that suggest an Afro-Venezuelan context, but these words do not appear to be grounded in the linguistic reality of the group they attempt to interpret.

As a member of the Vanguard Generation in Venezuela, Manuel Rodríguez Cárdenas made a singular contribution to the national literature. His importance is summed up by Pedro Díaz Seijas: "He is the initiator in our poetry of a thematics based in folklore, in life, in the customs of black Venezuelans. His book *Drum* is related to the black poetry of the continent represented by Nicolás Guillén, Emilio Ballagas and Jorge Artel."[8] Rodríguez Cárdenas is situated more toward the end of the spectrum occupied by Ballagas than the positions held by Guillén and Artel; as a literary pioneer, Manuel Rodríguez Cárdenas issued a thematic challenge that was not answered until four decades later.

Most of the controversy and negative criticism generated when *Drum* was first published was due to the fact that Venezuelans were not accustomed to having blacks occupy center stage, even as literary protagonists. Given the times and the customs in Venezuela at that historical juncture, this book was indeed a bold statement by Rodríguez Cárdenas. The critical hysteria precluded close readings of these poems, which would have revealed then, as now, that the author's ideological thrust was in tune with national norms that stressed ethnic movement toward the miscegenated center.

8. *La antigua y la moderna literatura venezolana: Estudio histórico-crítico, con antología*, 658.

4

Antonio Acosta Márquez

Yo pienso aquí donde . . . Estoy:
On Being and Not Being Black in Venezuela

Pardo/*mulato*/*mestizo* writers such as Ramón Díaz Sánchez and Manuel Rodríguez Cárdenas may have been ambivalent in their attitudes toward Afro-Venezuelans, but there is no doubt as to the intent of one of the most recent poetic affirmations of *negritud* in Venezuela. *I Think Right Here Where . . . I Am* by Antonio Acosta Márquez contains a statement by the author entitled "Un país donde los nuevos valores somos marginados" ("A Country Where under the New Values We Are Marginal"), in which he laments:

> Me llena de profunda tristeza editar este mi primer poemario fuera de mi patria. Fuera de mi gente. Lejos de los bosques de mi Barlovento. A millares de kilómetros de San José de Guaribe, lindo pueblo llanero que me vio crecer entre verdor de sabanas y mugir lastimeros de reses sedientas en los meses de veranos guariqueños.
> Me resulta sumamente lastimoso no haberlo editado en mi país; donde nacieron estos versos. Donde ellos vinieron hasta mí para que le rimara con el canto sublime y melancólico de la soiola.[1]

> (It fills me with profound sadness to edit this, my first book of poems outside of my homeland. Away from my people. Far from the forests of my Barlovento. Thousands of kilometers from San José de Guaribe, pretty plains town which saw me grow up amid the greenness of the savannas and the pitiful mooing of thirsty cattle in the Guaribe summer months.
> It makes me very sad not having edited it in my country, where

---

1. *Yo pienso aquí donde . . . Estoy,* iii. Further citations will be made parenthetically in the text. Unless otherwise noted, references in this chapter are to the first (1977) edition.

these verses were born. Where they came to me so that I would
rhyme them with the sublime and melancholy song of the flute.)

Acosta Márquez conveys the sentiment that his self-imposed exile
at that time was not voluntary, that there were obstacles other than
financial ones that prevented his book from being published in Venezuela. The resistance encountered by Acosta Márquez is not much
different from what happened to Rodríguez Cárdenas. The latter's
work was published and harshly criticized, while the former's was
met with silence. There is a basic difference, though, in the approach to the conception and elaboration of the poetry itself by the
authors.

In the prologue to *I Think Right Here Where . . . I Am*, entitled "Un
poeta del pueblo" (A Poet of the People), Anibal Nazoa writes:

> Antonio's poems are charged with the best feelings of the popular
> class of Venezuela: Love, Rebellion, Honesty, Clarity, Hatred of
> the oppressors. There does not exist in it the intention of saying
> something, of giving a content and an importance, we are almost
> tempted to say a revolutionary usefulness to each verse. For that
> reason, although at times his meter may not satisfy completely the
> demands of the craft, his rhythm invites me to convert them into a
> song, and we do not believe ourselves wrong by thinking that it
> was precisely to be sung that Antonio wrote these poems. (i)

The poems of Antonio Acosta Márquez are folk-based and rooted in
the Afro-Venezuelan popular oral tradition. They contain themes
familiar to the majority of people, and they are expressed in an
intelligible idiom, using registers that the people can comprehend.
The clarity of Acosta Márquez's expression should not be interpreted as a lack of sophistication, however, because he displays a
deep understanding of form and content relationships in treating
love, rebellion, ethnicity, honesty, clarity, and the hatred of the
oppressor.

In the tradition of Juan Pablo Sojo, *I Think Right Here Where . . . I
Am* is an affirmation of Afro-Venezuelan culture. It is a collection of
human, popular poems which express serious social concerns. The
plight of blacks throughout the Barlovento region provides the basis
for a culturalist assessment of the idea of an African past, the culture's linguistic and thematic survivals, its folk beliefs, its criticism
of injustice, and its development of an Afrocentric worldview.

This volume consists of forty-five selections which vary in form
and content and follow both the popular and the learned traditions.
At the core of this poetry is a sense of estrangement, of both phys-

ical and spiritual loss. By solidly grounding his work in the experiences of the people, Acosta Márquez is able to achieve a sense of authenticity that has been absent in many Venezuelan *negrista* writings. The amazing thing about this book is that it expresses precisely what many scholars maintain does not exist: an awareness by the people of Barlovento of their blackness.[2] A brief analysis of representative selections will reveal both the human dimension of Acosta Márquez's poems and his importance in maintaining an Afro-Venezuelan discourse.

It is appropriate to begin this discussion with "Canto a los Barloventeños" ("Song to the People of Barlovento"), since in this poem the poet presents an overview of his people and their relationship to Venezuelan society. This is one of several poems that interpret the region and attempt to come to grips with many of the inconsistencies and incongruities faced by a people whose life is a daily struggle for survival. This poem is the most positive of the lot:

> Negritos Barloventeños
> negritos de mi País
> los de aplastada nariz
> con puro sabor costeño
> Negritos como el carbón
> alegres y discharacheros
> de origen muy parranderos
> y de un gran corazón.
> Desde Caucagua a Juan Día
> se ven por los caminos
> cantando versos a lo divino
> Cantando minas y fulias
> Algunos se ven sufriendo
> con tristeza y amargura
> frente a la miseria dura
> que allá nos va destruyendo
> Ay, negritos Barloventeños!
> De Riochico a Panaquire

2. This assertion has been reinforced recently by Max Hans Brandt in his doctoral thesis, "An Ethnomusicological Study of Three Afro-Venezuelan Drum Ensembles of Barlovento." Regarding the perception of Barlovento as a piece of Africa, Winthrop R. Wright has written: "The region's black residents have become exotic and peripheral people; the national press treats them as curiosities, victims of disasters, or subjects of quaint human interest stories. Somehow, Barlovento lingers on as a land inhabited by happy-go-lucky descendants of slaves, who still speak African dialects, eat African food and maintain African culture" (*Café con leche: Race, Class and National Image in Venezuela*, 127–28).

desde el Guapo hasta Guatire
los ricos son nuestros dueños
Negrito de Barlovento
de piel color de carbón
ya toda mi inspiración
se va con tus pensamientos
Negritos de mi región
Sembradores, pescadores
y también agricultores
que están en mi población
gentes sinceras y honestas;
hijos de la explotación
A los negros y las negritas
de mi región tan querida
les ofrezco a ustedes mi vida
de Riochico a la Palmita
Dándoles estas rimas sencillas
aunque no son muy bonitas.
                                    (3)

(Black people of Barlovento
black people of my Country
those with a flat nose
with pure coastal flavor
Blacks like coal
happy and easy going
of very festive origins
and with a great heart.
From Caucagua to Juan Día
you are seen along the roads
singing heavenly verses
Singing worldly songs
Some are seen suffering
with sadness and bitterness
faced with the harsh misery
which is destroying us
Oh, black people of Barlovento!
From Riochico to Panaquire
from Guapo to Guatire
the rich are our owners
Barlovento blacks
with skin the color of coal
already all my inspiration
goes with your thoughts
Blacks of my region
Planters and fishermen
and also farmers

who are in my town
sincere and honest people;
children of exploitation
To the black men and women
of my beloved region
I offer you my life
from Riochico to Palmita
giving you these simple rhymes
although they're not very pretty.)

In this cultural preamble to the volume, the poet creates the perception that the Barloventeños are an optimistic people who are trapped
in a social system designed to take advantage of their many positive
qualities. This has been so historically, and it is still a situation that
does not bode well for the future. There is a dialectical process at
work in the poem, since on the one hand the poet is affirming the
shared, learned behavior of the blacks, while on the other hand he
views the reality of daily life: "singing worldly songs / Some are
seen suffering / with sadness and bitterness / faced with the harsh
misery / which is destroying us." The reason for their plight is clear:
"the rich people are our owners." The idea of the black population
of Barlovento as a dependent, exploited entity is repeated fre-
quently throughout this volume. The poet is not merely singing the
praises of the people but also expressing a need for change by artic-
ulating their circumstances.

The poet presents Afro-Venezuelan culture as being defined and
distilled within the context of Barlovento's ceremonies and celebrations. This is apparent in the selection "Tradiciones Barloventeñas"
("Traditions of Barlovento"), in which the drum culture and its relationship to the Festival of St. John the Baptist are scrutinized. In this
poem, Acosta Márquez mines the same cultural intertext as Juan
Pablo Sojo in *Black St. John's Eve,* in which the narrator exclaims,
"¡La gran voz del viejo *mina*! ¡Voz del ancestro congregando el clan!
Voz misteriosa, que reclama su sangre africana, su resto de sangre
africana perdida en los recovecos de las venas como vaga reminis-
cencia. . . ." (The great voice of the mina drum! Ancestral voice
congregating the clan! Mysterious voice which reclaims its African
blood, its remainder of African blood lost in the recesses of the
veins as a vague reminiscence).[3] The atmosphere in the poem "Traditions of Barrlovento" bears an intertextual relationship to Sojo's
work. In this poem the first two stanzas set the tone:

3. *Nochebuena negra,* 300.

I

Están afinando la curveta,
las minas y el tambor,
se prepara halagador,
Barlovento para sus fiestas.
Y cuando llega la fiesta,
a la que tanto han nombrado,
todo el mundo alborotado,
entra a sonar la curveta.

II

La noche ya se avecina;
a la fiesta todos van,
a cantarle a San Juan,
a la población vecina.
Está la mina sonando,
la noche buena de San Juan.
a la mina también le dan,
palos mientras van cantando.

(17)

I

(They're tuning the *curveta*,
the *minas* and the *tambor*,
Barlovento is really dressed up,
for its celebrations.
And when the celebration begins,
about which there has been so much talk,
everybody excitedly,
enters to the sound of the *curveta*.

II

The night already approaches;
everybody goes to the fiesta,
to sing to St. John,
in the neighboring town.
The *mina* is announcing,
St. John's Eve.
they also lend to the *mina*,
strokes as they are singing.)

In his discussion of the importance of drums in Afro-Venezuelan music, Alfredo Chacón, cited earlier in this study, refers to Luis Felipe Ramón y Rivera, who has studied African remnants in that culture. Chacón observes

among the most significant: the undeniable transfer to our soil of melodic and rhythmic African elements; the African origin of cer-

tain musical instruments, especially drums; and the importance
of oral communication in the original fixation of African drums in
Venezuela. . . . The *cumacos, tamunangos, redondos, mina,* and *curbata* drums along with the *maracas,* the *palos* or *laures* and the *gua-
rura* are instruments utilized during the celebration of St. John.[4]

These are percussion instruments that are integral components of
Afro-Venezuelan culture and have specific functions. The *curbata* or
curveta, for instance, usually serves as a companion to the *mina* in
performance. In the poem, these drums and the *palos* used to strike
them play a prominent role. "Traditions of Barlovento" succeeds in
capturing the emotions, sights, and sounds associated with the ceremonies devoted to Saint John the Baptist, which is one of the most
traditional and most significant of all Afro-Venezuelan celebrations
and represents the syncretism of Spanish Catholicism and African
cultural practices.

The overall significance of the drum culture and its relationship to
ancestrality is the most important factor in the poem, however. As
Josaphat B. Kubayanda points out, "Ancestrality makes the spoken
word come to life in any oral creative endeavor. . . . That word
sometimes has to do with drum language, itself the sacred, sonic
idiom of completion and continuity with the ancient world of one's
tropical forebearers."[5] Afro-Venezuelan writers such as Sojo and
Acosta Márquez certainly recognize this important aspect of the
African past, and they do not present all ceremonial rituals as fun
and games. The recurring presence of drums and their relationship
to orality and ancestrality in Acosta Márquez's poems are manifestations of the type of cultural continuity envisioned by the poet.

The darker side of Barlovento is expressed, however, in the poem
"Noche de Barlovento" ("Night of Barlovento"). This selection interprets impending death, which is presented through the use of
dark metaphors and a negative metonymic environment.

Negra la noche,
la negra noche de Barlovento . . .
La negra llora,
la negra gime,

4. *Poblaciones y culturas negras de Venezuela,* 61.
5. "Notes on the Impact of African Oral-Tradition Rhetoric on Latin-American and
Caribbean Writing," 6. Wright observes, regarding this celebration: "During the
past few decades white Venezuelans have participated in the celebration of major
Afro-Venezuelan holidays, such as St. John the Baptist's day on June 24. . . . On this
holiday, and several others, whites readily join blacks and *pardos* in acclaiming part
of their nation's African heritage" (*Café con leche,* 127).

el negrito llora,
ella le riñe.
Canta el Aruco,
en el sarrapial,
luego el negrito,
vuelve a llorar.
                    (4)

(Black is the night,
the black night of Barlovento . . .
The black woman cries,
the black woman moans,
the black child cries,
she scolds him.
The Aruco sings,
in the thicket,
then the black child,
begins to cry again.)

Analogous to its appearance in Sojo's work, the Aruco presages death, since within the black culture of Barlovento, according to Acosta Márquez, "the country people believe it is an incarnation of evil spirits" (97). The initial verses of the poem dramatize a situation of suffering between mother and son. Then, the motif of "the black night of Barlovento" and variations thereof symbolize both the internal and external struggles that are occurring. The stormy night has brought flooding and the plague as well as a negatively harmonious natural environment of owls, singing crickets, and attacking mosquitoes. The internal anguish and suffering, coupled with a hostile metaphoric ambience, culminates in tragedy: "Mientras la noche, / ya va cayendo, / la negra llora, / porque el negrito / —Se está muriendo" (While the night, / is already falling, / the black woman cries / because the little black child / —is dying; 5). Death occurs within the negative symbolism that structures modes of belief in Barlovento.

The decline of the entire Barlovento region is forecasted in "Ocaso de Barlovento" ("Death of Barlovento"):

Montañas vírgenes
        Cacaotales,
El viento sopla
        en los cocales.
Sonrisa de un negro
        blanco los dientes.

Si canta el Aruco
    viene la muerte.
Senderos tristes
    pies enlodados.
Rancho de palma,
    negro angustiado.
Si el Mina no suena
    no hay curveta.
Ya el negro no canta
    triste se acuesta.
Se desbordan los ríos
    siembra inundada.
El negro agricultor
    no tiene ni azada.
Sin el tamborero
    muere el velorio.
Los zancudos rondan
    el dormitorio.
Ya no canta nadie
    no hay alegría.
Y los negros lloran
    noches tras días.
Los negros tristes
    no saben reir
Mi Barlovento agoniza
    se nos va a morir.
       (89–90)

(Virgin mountains
    Cacao plantations,
The wind blows
    in the berry bushes.
The smile of a black
    with white teeth.
If the Aruco sings
    death comes.
Sad trails
    muddy feet.
Straw houses,
    suffering blacks.
If the *mina* doesn't sound
    there is no *curveta*.
The black sings no more
    goes to bed sad.
The rivers overflow
    harvest flooded.

The black farmer
    has no plow.
Without the drummer
    the wake dies.
Mosquitos surround
    the bedroom.
Nobody sings now
    there is no happiness.
And the blacks cry
    nights after days.
The sad blacks
    don't know how to smile
My Barlovento agonizes
    It's going to die on us.)

The ironic notion evident in this poem is that the culture and environment of blacks in Barlovento are not enough to sustain them in the face of overwhelming social and economic odds. Negative imagery underscores the economic demise of the region during a poignant reflection upon a depressing present.

In *I Think Right Here Where . . . I Am,* there is a very forceful autobiographical dimension and a firm identification between the poet and his people. "Esta es mi gente" ("This Is My People"), "Pueblo mió" ("My Town"), and "El consejo de mi padre" ("The Advice of My Father") are indicative of these tendencies. "This Is My People" is structured around a series of rhetorical questions designed to elicit a response to the plight of the masses:

¿Mi gente?
¿Cúal gente?
Esta es mi gente . . .
La que vive de las sobras
que nos dejan los pudientes
la que procría hijos desnutridos
la que es explotada por pervertidos
¿Mi gente?
Esta es mi gente
La que de un mundo mejor
le habla a los oprimidos
La que prepara a las masas
contra el burgúes delincuente.
                    (20)

(My people?
Which people?

This is my people . . .
Those who live off the crumbs
that the powerful leave us
those who raise malnourished children
those who are exploited by perverts
My people?
This is my people
Those who about a better world
talk to the oppressed
Those who prepare the masses
against the irresponsible bourgeoisie.)

His people, those who suffer, cry, and struggle in the present, which seems to be a part of a never-ending past, are portrayed as victims of an uncaring social process. The exploited, malnourished children of today are not equipped to function positively in the future. The poet views the real problem as being rooted in class tensions between the haves and the have-nots, and he identifies strongly with those who act as agents for change. There is an implicit call for revolutionary advancement in this poem, perhaps through overt resistance.

"The Advice of My Father" is told from the perspective of a son (the poet) who reacts to the brutalizing of his father (Pedro Acosta Machado) at the hands of the authorities (friends of the government). Apparently, the father's crime is being defiant and disrespectful of the status quo and making his political views known. The poet reminisces over the scene in which his father is taken away by the forces of law and order:

Pero aquel humilde negro
y de tan gran corazón
sin importarle el martirio
gritaba de indignación
—¡ABAJO LA DICTADURA
VIVA LA REVOLUCION!!
(26)

(But that humble black man
with such great heart
without martyrdom mattering
shouted out his indignation
—DOWN WITH THE DICTATORSHIP
LONG LIVE THE REVOLUTION!!)

Pedro Acosta Machado, humble but brave, is apparently killed by the authorities for his heroic posture of resistance. His call for a revolution, a complete change in the social and economic systems, has a profound impact upon the poet:

> Luego mi padre me vio
> y relampagueó la vista,
> —¡VES HIJO PARA QUE APRENDA,
> A SER UN BUEN SOCIALISTA!
> Así me gritó mi padre,
> bajo los golpes fascistas.
>
> (27)

> (Then my father saw me
> and flashing me a glance,
> —LOOK SON IN ORDER TO LEARN
> TO BE A GOOD SOCIALIST!
> Thus my father shouted to me,
> beneath the fascist blows.)

The atrocities committed against his family for the sake of maintaining the status quo remain riveted in the poet's imagination. They serve not only as the motivating force behind his social views but also as inspiration for his verses that are critical of the country's owners, who maintain the masses near the starvation level.

"My Town," dedicated "To the humble of my town," is a chronicle of cultural loss, a search for identity and solidarity. San Antonio is evoked as a "Pueblito de Barlovento, por tus hijos abandonado, víctima del poderío / del que vive holgadamente, pueblo agonizante" (Little town of Barlovento, abandoned by its children, victim of wealth / of one who lives leisurely, an agonizing town; 23). Images of loss, abandonment, estrangement, and disregard abound as San Antonio is respected neither by its own inhabitants nor by those who seek to exploit its human and natural resources.

> San Antonio pueblo mío,
> con tus calles llenas de rocío,
> sin asfalta, ni cemento
> eres otro pueblo olvidado en mi Barlovento.
> Tus fiestas patronales ahora "Ferias,"
> no nos dicen nada, en ti sigue la miseria.
> Sigue la callecita aquella: la de la entrada
> llena de huecos, fango y mal engransonada.
> Y para entrar al dispensario rural
> se pasan por barriales ¡TODO SIGUE IGUAL!
> En lo que ha cambiado gigantescamente
> es que tiene tres negocios de venta de aguardiente

con tan pocos habitantes casi cuatro gatos
hay bares a montones, pero ni un abasto.
(24)

(San Antonio my town,
with your streets filled with dew,
without asphalt or cement
you are another forgotten town of my Barlovento.
Your saint's day festivals now "Fairs,"
they don't say anything to us, in you misery continues.
Follow that little street: the one at the entrance
full of holes, mud and badly kept.
And to enter the rural dispensary
one passes through barricades EVERYTHING REMAINS THE SAME!
What has changed gigantically
is that there are three liquor stores
with so few inhabitants almost four whore houses
there are many bars, but not one grocery store.)

The physical decline of San Antonio is mirrored in its moral decay. Alcohol, bars, and prostitution provide an escape and a diversion for some of the people trapped in a set of social and economic circumstances where EVERYTHING REMAINS THE SAME!

Only the poet remains optimistic:

San Antonio amigo: "Cúanto lo siento"
pero tarde o temprano se acabarán tus sufrimientos
y entonces si cambiará tu cara
esperemos pueblo mío, la nueva alborada.
(25)

(San Antonio friend: "How sorry I am"
but sooner or later your suffering will end
and then yes your face will change
let's wait my town, for the new dawn.)

This poignant, emotional selection exemplifies the relentless search by the poet for the metaphorical center of his existence and that of his people. The ongoing process of deculturation has taken an enormous physical and psychological toll upon individuals and objects most dear to him. An eternal optimist, the poet's "new dawn" will be a future of human equality, economic justice, and self-assuredness for Afro-Venezuelans.

Another concern of this volume is the spiritual well-being of the people. Regarding the magical religious elements that characterize

Afro-Venezuelan communities, Alfredo Chacón notes that "currently the name *curanderismo* [folk healing] is used to designated beliefs and practices of good intention and *brujería* [witchcraft] for evil intentions. In both cases the corresponding ritualistic acts are linked to the Catholic religion through the saying of certain prayers and the invocation of saints and other sacred figures."[6]

This type of *supportive* ritual practice is evident in the poem "Relafica de la casa embrujada" ("Prayer for the Bewitched House"), which is an invocation of benign spirits to combat evil. It is structured around a chorus, an incantation, and a call and response, all used to alleviate the situation. The poem begins:

CORO
TUMBA LA CASA PACHECO
TUMBALA, TUMBALA, TUMBALA.
TUMBA LA CASA PACHECO
QUETA CASA TA EMBRUJA. (bis)

A negro ooo . . . ven pa cá
acélcate pa ete rincon
que te voy a jumá el tabaco
y te voy a rezar la oración
Gua, arrímate pasia el altal
que voy acé la invocación
primero me he de pelsinal
y depué rezo la oración.

(9)

(CHORUS
KNOCK DOWN THE PACHECO HOUSE
KNOCK IT DOWN, KNOCK IT DOWN, KNOCK IT DOWN.
KNOCK DOWN THE PACHECO HOUSE
BECAUSE IT IS BEWITCHED. (repeat)

Black people . . . come here
come close to this corner
because I'm going to smoke tobacco
and say a prayer for you
Come on, approach the altar
because I'm going to say the invocation
first I have to bow
and afterward say a prayer.)

Spoken in popular language, the chorus opens and brings closure to the ritual, which is filled with popular interpretations and de-

6. *Poblaciones y culturas*, 65.

signed to exorcise evil. The ceremonial smoke and prayer precede the summoning of powerful spirits to right the wrong that has been done. Then a ritualistic cleansing of the house is in order.

The exact nature of the evil is revealed in the third stanza, where it is stated that an omen has been buried in the middle of the corridor. Apparently, Tomasa Pérez is the culprit who has bewitched the house. Of this practice, known as *patuco*, the editors of *I Think Right Here Where . . . I Am* write that "it is also said that certain bewitching potions are assembled with the name, surname and a picture of the targeted person. They also use a rag doll and bury it in a determined place" (102). "Prayer for the Bewitched House" interprets the spirit of mistrust and apprehension associated with the contaminated house and its impact upon the psychology of the village. At the same time, its conception is within the realm of what is believed to be the Afro-Venezuelan magical thought and practice of this particular region.

The issues of nationhood and ethnicity are raised in the poem "¿Qué color tiene mi Patria?" ("What Color is My Homeland?"). The poet is consistent in his portrayal of social inequities based primarily upon color and class. Through a series of rhetorical questions, he reiterates the point:

¿Qué color tiene mi Patria?
Nunca, nunca lo sabré
porque yo que soy tu hijo
jamás a tí te venderé.
¿Qué color tiene mi Patria?
Yo lo quisiera saber
¿Por qué tus hijos te venden?
Acaso por ser mujer?
(33)

(What color is my Homeland?
Never, never will I know
because I who am your son
never will I sell you.
What color is my Homeland?
I would like to know
Why your children sell you?
Perhaps because you are a woman?)

The poet criticizes here those who respect only money and place financial gain ahead of nationalism and loyalty to the majority of the people. Color prejudice and attitudes of superiority are important components of this mindset. There is the strong prostitution analogy, which suggests pillage by outsiders who also discriminate:

> Antes tú eras cobriza,
> del color de las hojas secas,
> luego llegaron los blancos
> te pusieron blanca y negra.
> Hasta los que van naciendo
> van cambiando tu color,
> lo que viene de otras partes
> siempre para ellos es mejor.
> No aprecian tu tradición
> se olvidan tu folklor
>
> (33)

> (Before you were bronze,
> the color of dry leaves,
> then the whites came
> they made you black and white.
> Even those who are being born
> are changing your color,
> that which comes from other places
> is always better for them.
> They don't appreciate your tradition
> they forget your folklore.)

The poet views the imposition of European values and the de-emphasizing of African norms as a major problem, from a human perspective, in Venezuela. The outsiders bring their prejudices and superiority complexes, which work to the disadvantage of black indigenous culture. This type of cultural brainwashing favors the foreign over the native and looks abroad for direction. The result is cultural imposition that alienates and destroys from within. On a biological level, there is pressure for the miscegenated masses to become even lighter.

The poem "Soliloquio de el Negro Fulia" ("Soliloquy of the Black Fulia") addresses alienation from the perspective of blacks, who feel profoundly the erosion of their culture. *Fulias* are songs traditionally sung at funerals, but here the demise is more encompassing. The loss has occurred in the areas of dance ("ahora ni lo viejo / bailan el joropo"; now not even the old people / dance the joropo), dress ("ahora usan zapato / con piel de gamuza"; now they wear shoes / with suede), and food ("ahora se usa / harina pre-cosia"; now they use / pre-cooked meal). This cultural erosion is caused by the *gringo,* whose influence must be stopped and local customs reaffirmed:

> Que siga la fulia
> que siga la tambora
> que viendo eta cosa
> mi corazón llora
> que no siga mi pueblo
> amando lo ajeno
> que no siga fumando
> y tomando veneno
> que no siga mi gente
> tan pegao a lo gringo
> yo contra ello lucho
> y nunca me rindo
> si muere el folklor
> y la tradición
> peldemo la Patria
> no habrá liberación.
>   (13)

> (Let the song flow
> let the drum peal
> by seeing this thing
> my heart cries
> don't let my people continue
> loving foreign things
> don't let them continue smoking
> and drinking poison
> don't let my people continue
> so glued to the *gringo*
> I will fight against that
> and never surrender
> if folklore
> and tradition dies and
> we lose the Homeland
> there will be no liberation.)

The specter of the exploitative *gringo* is raised again as the poet pleads for reason and the reaffirmation of cultural values in the face of gross materialism. The mythic homeland that he has created is the black ancestral region of Barlovento, the center that is being eroded.

At the core of the problem of the deafricanization of Venezuelan cultures, especially in traditionally black areas such as Barlovento, is the migration to Caracas. The poet's concern is evident in his lament for San Antonio and other poems throughout the collection. The sense of displacement, alienation, and cultural estrangement is undoubtedly his primary thematic concern.

"Relafica de el Negro y la Hija Ausente" ("Prayer of the Black Man and His Absent Daughter"), a dramatic poem in popular verse, explores this topic from the perspective of the poor in the form of call and response. "Where is your daughter?" and "She has left and will never return" set the tone for the exchange. The father's response is that his daughter left for economic reasons and works as a maid, a cook, a waitress, and a prostitute. She lives a lie that is finally discovered by her father, who responds bitterly:

> Polque el Gringo jue el culpable
> y la mala situación
> que me llevó a mi negrita
> camino a la perdición
> La miseria aquí en mi región
> que solo e calamidá
> no llena de frutración
> y emigramos a la ciudá
>
> (16)
>
> (Because the Gringo was the guilty one
> and the bad situation
> which took away my little black girl
> en route to ruination
> The misery here in my region
> which is only calamity
> fills us with frustration
> and we emigrate to the city)

There is an out-migration from the region which has devastating human and social consequences. The image "se enlodó" ("soiled") to describe Asunción's—his daughter's—plight is an extended metaphor for the situation in the city in which many become dirtied and bogged down in an inescapable urban environment. Asunción has been exploited in menial jobs, impregnated, and abandoned. Certainly, she cannot return home again as a principle of honor and respect to the family and to herself.

Exploitation of the poor worker is a concern of the poet expressed in poems such as "Soliloquio de un obrero" ("Soliloquy of a Worker") and "Canto para obrero" ("Song for the Worker"). These two selections are indicative of the volume's popular bent, which relates events from the perspective of the oppressed. In "Soliloquy of a Worker," the attitude is that of a slave:

Negra, soy obrero
y además soy explotado
soy obrero esclavizado
mi patrón es un negrero
para ganarme el dinero
pa comprarte la comida
se me hacen hondas heridas
en mi ennegrecido cuero.

(34)

(Black Woman, I am a worker
and besides I'm exploited
I am an enslaved worker
my boss is a slave driver
in order to earn money
to buy you food
they make deep wounds
in my blackened hide.)

"Exploited," "enslaved," and "blackened" are highly charged ad-
jectives that effectively convey the situation of an exploited person
trapped without recourse in a system designed to exact maximum
benefits for the *patrón*.

The poem's three stanzas capture succinctly the dilemma of an
individual who is semiliterate but who is well schooled in the ways
of the world and envisions a better day for himself and his people.
Exploitation and abuse have not destroyed his spirit and survival
instinct.

The same mixture of present-day suffering and future optimism
is carried over into the poem "Song for the Worker." Written in the
popular *décima* form, it too is filled with pain and suffering:

Llanto de pecho cansado,
que desde la infancia amarga,
ves que la esperanza es larga,
y te has hecho un desdichado.
Porque nunca ha mejorado,
a pesar de las promesas,
tu tristeza es más tristeza,
y tu miseria es el doble.
Cada día te haces más pobre,
por darle a otros riquezas

(43)

(The cry of a tired breast,
which since bitter infancy,

you see that hope is long,
and you have become a wretch.
Because things haven't improved,
in spite of the promises,
your sadness is more sadness,
and your misery is double.
Each day you became poorer,
in order to give others riches)

The worker is part of a negative historical process that has yielded
diminishing returns. Hope and promises have resulted in only double misery, further entrenching black workers in a condition of dependency. Nevertheless, they are urged to struggle and fraternize
"Por lo que puede pasar" (For what can happen; 44).

As we have seen, the plight of women is an important concern of
this volume. They are not presented as sex objects or dancing ma-
chines, but in many cases as those who bear the brunt of discrimi-
natory practices in an uncaring society. "Décimas a las madres
trabajadoras" ("*Décimas* to Working Mothers") and "A madres aban-
donadas" ("To Abandoned Mothers") are selections that treat these
issues. The first of these poems is constructed, ironically, around
the celebration of Mother's Day:

Madre tú no estás alegre,
tu día están celebrando,
sigue pegada a la alteza
trabajando y trabajando.
Otras madres andan gozando,
sobre todo las burguesas,
tu sufrir no les interesa,
ni el por qué tú no descanzas.
En ti murió la esperanza,
tu tristeza es más tristeza
                    (21)

(Mother you are not happy,
they're celebrating your day,
you continue attached to royalty
working and working.
Other mothers enjoy themselves,
especially the bourgeoisie,
your suffering doesn't interest them,
nor the reason you don't rest.
In you hope died,
Your sadness is more sadness)

The initial depressing image, which effectively mocks any pretense this mother may have of celebrating "her" day, is sustained throughout the poem. Portrayed as a victim whose lot in life is "working and working," responsibility for this situation is placed squarely with the class structure in which one segment, the bourgeoisie, perceives the other as being there to make life more enjoyable for them and their habits. Hopelessness, alienation, and a profound sadness spiritually exacerbate a situation of physical and economic exploitation.

The impact of seduction, abandonment, and subsequent poverty upon women is the theme of "To Abandoned Mothers":

> A ti madre engañada,
> la de los hijos sin padres
> que por amor fuiste madre,
> pero luego abandonada.
> Tú que fuiste seducida,
> por un malvado cretino,
> que te guió al mal camino,
> haciéndote una perdida.
> (48)

> (To you deceived mother,
> the one with children without fathers
> who for love was a mother,
> but soon abandoned.
> You who were seduced,
> by a no-good cretin,
> who guided you down the evil path,
> making you a lost one.)

"Deceived," "abandoned," "seduced," and "lost" are terms that underscore the reality of a group of people whose chances for success in the society are marginal at best. Although the males who exploit her are characterized negatively and cast generally in a bad light, the woman is left to bear the consequences in the fight for survival.

> Trabajas como tendera
> quizás como cortadora
> o de humilde planchadora,
> o tal vez de mesonera,
> Quizás eres barrendera
> tal vez seas boticaria,

o una linda secretaria
o una gorda cocinera
(50)

(You work as a shopkeeper
perhaps as a seamstress
or a humble ironer,
or perhaps an innkeeper,
Perhaps you are a street sweeper
maybe even a pharmacist,
or a beautiful secretary
or a fat cook.)

Her destiny is by no means certain as the anaphora of "or," "perhaps," and "maybe" exacerbate the degree of uncertainty that is implicit in this poem. Since the woman's destiny is so tightly bound to that of the man, her tenuous situation is twice as problematic.

The last of the volume's mother poems is entitled "Madre" (Mother") and so dedicated. This poignant remembrance is not characterized by the harshness so evident in the preceding two selections. Instead, "Mother" is a type of repentance for the poet's not fully appreciating her value. The contrast between then and now is striking:

¡Madre, eres dulce y comprensiva
amena y complaciente,
personificas la ternura,
la sensibilidad! ¡Y eres paciente!
. . . .
Madre cuando te tenemos viva,
te miramos con indiferencia,
te hacemos sufrir en carne propia,
por no tener paciencia,
y cuando nos vas a dar un consejo,
uno siempre lo desprecia.
(90)

(Mother, you are sweet and understanding
pleasant and obliging,
you personify tenderness,
sensibility and you are patient!
. . . .
Mother while we have you alive,
we look at you with indifference,
we make you suffer in the flesh,
by not having patience,
and when you are going to give us advice,
one always dislikes it.)

"Mother" raises a basic human dilemma regarding respect for and appreciation of the mother, who bears the brunt of family tension and pressure. Little heed is paid to her wise counsel in life, but after she is gone regrets reign. In this poem, too, the poet conveys the sad but true message that in his society women are born to suffer both at the hands of strangers and their own kind.

The specter of death weighs heavily upon the population of Barlovento. Poems like "Lamento negro a la muerte" ("Black Lament for Death"), "Velorio de cruz y tambores" ("A Cross and Drum Wake"), "Décima de tristeza y llanto" ("*Décima* of Sadness and Crying"), "Adiós a Benito Quiroz" ("Goodbye to Benito Quiroz"), "Adiós a Quintín Duarte" ("Goodbye to Quintín Duarte"), and others recount both the demise of black culture and of popular figures who have left their mark historically upon the region.

"Black Lament for Death" is an elegy on the death of a daughter that captures the suffering of her father. It begins:

ALATEE, BILITU, VE
A LATE, A LA TE,
BIBLITU, VE, ALATE,
MI NEGRITA SE ME FUE.

En aquel rancho de palma,
ubicado allá en Tapipa,
lloraba el negro Tomás,
la muerte de su negrita.
(5)

(In that hut of palms,
located over there in Tapipa,
Thomas the Black was mourning,
the death of his little black girl.)

The choral beginning takes on added significance because "Alatee," according to the author, is a "palabra de un canto utilizado por los antiguos esclavos de ciertas localidades de Barlovento, cuando iban a enterrar a un doliente, cuyo significado hasta hoy es desconocido" (word from a song utilized by the old slaves of certain sections of Barlovento, when they were going to bury a dying person, whose meaning today is unknown; 97). In effect, the people are calling upon African ritual to ease the transition from the world of the living to that of the ancestors. Tomás's response is within the popular black tradition in regard to the presence of the Aruco bird; in addition, Tomás utilizes local linguistic registers. Both of these techniques are employed by Acosta Márquez in other poems.

The atmosphere of the wake, as ritual, is captured magnificently in the poem "A Cross and Drum Wake."

El patio se tá llenando
llegan gente de Ríochico
Del Guapo y de San Fernando
Ya vide a la negra Juana
quel pecho se tá aclarando
Así se toca negro José
la tambora de pua qui

. . . .
Aunque me vean así
negro bemba colorá
la tradición de mi tierra
ya no la puedo olvidá
¡NUNCA OLVIDARE LO MIO
NI LO AJENO E DE IMITA!

(8)

(The patio is filling up
people arrive from Ríochico
From Guapo and San Fernando
you can already see black Juana
who is getting fixed up
Black José is playing
the calling drum

. . . .
Although I look this way
a thick lipped black
the tradition of my land
I cannot forget
I WILL NEVER FORGET MINE
NOR IS THE FOREIGN TO BE IMITATED!)

In this instance, ritual is combined with social message in an effort to affirm adherence to Afro-Venezuelan values in Barlovento. Hopefully, the physical death will not always be replicated by a cultural demise.

Compassion is one of the motifs that recur throughout this volume. An expressed feeling of solidarity with the downtrodden and the abused comes to the fore in many of the poems already discussed, but it appears most forcefully in "The Beggar." According to the poet, this poem is based on the life of "Tapón," a popular beggar from the village of Catia. The initial scene of the poem is set as Tapón is being chased by a mob that wishes to do him bodily harm, and the narrator intervenes and takes the mob to task:

¿No se sienten ya felices?
¿Acaso les ha dado pena?
Gozen en la desgracia ajena,
quizás éste no fue así.
Mire, el hombre está aquí,
aunque está sucio el anciano,
yo lo toco con mis manos,
y hasta lo llamo mi amigo.
Para mí no es un mendigo,
para mí es un ser humano.
                                        (40)

(Don't you feel happy now?
Perhaps he has bothered you?
Enjoy the distant misfortune,
perhaps this one was not this way.
Look, the man is here,
although the old man is dirty,
I touch him with my hands,
I even call him my friend.
For me he is not a beggar,
For me he is a human being.)

The poet's intent is to humanize a dehumanized individual and to call into question some of society's negative attitudes toward the poor. The end result is positive, as the beggar tells his story and emerges with dignity and personal integrity in spite of his physical and economic circumstances.

The overwhelming compassion and love that the poet feels for his region and its people is summed up in the poem "Wind and Sea." Here, feeling is elevated to an existential level:

Mar de Higuerote, pintando
la angustia de Barlovento,
penas y tristezas de hijo,
que se va llevando el viento.
. . . .
Sufrir de un hombre de pueblo,
llanto amargo de un poeta,
que sufre al verte tan solo,
que de tí nadie se acuerda.
. . . .
¡Barlovento tierra mía!
llanto de un hombre que llora,
nadie ya de tí se acuerda,
amplia belleza de otrora.

. . . .
Región que han dejado sola.
triste y pobres están los pueblos,
donde nací un día cualquiera,
entre amarguras y desvelos.
                              (41–42)

(Sea of Higuerote, painting
the anguish of Barlovento,
pain and sadness of a child,
which the wind is carrying away.
. . . .
The suffering of a home boy,
the bitter cry of a poet,
who suffers upon seeing you so alone
nobody still remembers you.
. . . .
Barlovento my land!
the cry of a man who grieves,
nobody remembers you now,
spacious beauty of another time.
. . . .
Region they have left alone.
the people are sad and poor,
where I was born any old day,
among pain and shamelessness.)

Barlovento, the homeland, is the generator of a bittersweet individual experience. On the one hand, it lacks economic opportunities for blacks; on the other hand, it is the matrix from which
cultural continuity is generated. The poet's work is inextricably
bound to the context from whence he emerged, an environment
that has suffered an irrevocable human loss.

Pensar (think) is the unifying message of this volume. Blacks are encouraged not only to reflect upon their plight but also to use their brain
to begin fomenting positive actions. This is the situation set forth in
"Think Black Man Think" and "I Think Right Here Where . . . I Am."
The thrust of the first selection is affirmation and solidarity:

                    I
        Está acorralado el negro
    por el hambre y las miserias,
    en su faz se ve la angustia
    su tristeza y sus tragedias.
    Color de esperanza pobre
    negro, de torso desnudo,

obrero venezolano
hombre de trabajo rudo.

II
Negro, color de petroleo
Negro, color del café,
hombre de manos callosas,
hombre, de ampollas en los pies.
Hijo de una madre pobre
y de un padre cualquiera,
Negro, hijo abandonado
por un padre del sistema.

III
Hijo sin estudios buenos
porque en tu infancia truncada,
limpiaba zapatos, cuidabas carros
a las gentes adineradas.
Hoy Negro, que ya eres padre
eres un obrero sumiso,
¿por qué no alzas la frente?
Piensas que tienes tus hijos.

IV
Piensa siempre en el futuro
y en el bien de los demás,
piensa que otros no vivan
como tú viviendo está.
Es mejor pensar por todos
que ser uno individual,
deja de ser egoísta
piensa por el bien total.

(28)

I
(The black man is cornered
by hunger and misery,
in his face one sees the anguish
his sadness and his tragedies.
Color of hope poor
black, bare chested,
Venezuelan worker
man of manual labor.

II
Black, color of petroleum
Black, color of coffee,
man with calloused hands,
man with blisters on his feet.

Son of a poor mother
and of an unknown father,
Black, abandoned son
by a father of the system.

III
Son without good education
because in your shortened infancy,
you shined shoes, cared for cars
of the wealthy people.
Today Black Man, now that you are a father
you are a submissive worker,
why don't you lift up your head?
Think about what your children have.

IV
Think always about the future
and the well-being of the rest,
think so that others may not live
like you are living.
It's better to think for all
than to be one individual,
stop being egoistic
think for the total good.)

Trapped by both his color and his economic circumstances within an indifferent society, the black has very limited options. The negativity associated with being black and poor is emphasized in this poetic assessment of the color/class relationship. With a menial occupation, which abuses his body constantly, and ongoing psychological pressures, the black is a true orphan of the social and economic systems. Uneducated and condemned to menial occupations in the past, he is implored to resist in the present, so that in the future his children will be able to break the cycle of poverty, discrimination, and hopelessness. The black is reminded that his plight is shared by many others and only through collective action will there be a possibility of change for the better.

"I Think Right Here Where . . . I Am" is a poem that also amplifies the book's central metaphor interpreting the plight of blacks in Venezuela. A series of rhetorical questions pertaining to intelligence, personhood, and war precedes the principal issues of racism and discrimination that are raised in the poem:

Yo pienso aquí en donde estoy
en donde estoy yo pensando,
en mi raza tan sufrida.

Y por dondequiera que voy
salmuera les van echando,
a mis llagas y a mis heridas.

Jamás encuentro yo un consuelo
porque cargo está marca,
que no la puedo ocultar.
. . . .
Y hasta me ves con recelos
y con tus ojos me abarcas,
queriéndome estrangular.

Por esta senda que voy
por donde yo voy andando,
todo es triste y lastimoso.
. . . .
Yo pienso aquí en donde estoy
en donde estoy yo pensando,
que algún día tendremos un GOZO!
                                    (36)

(I think right here where I am
where I'm thinking,
about my long suffering race.

And wherever I go
they throw brine,
on my scars and wounds.

I will never find consolation
because I bear this mark,
that I cannot hide.
. . . .
You even look at me with disgust
and with your eyes you corner me,
wishing to strangle me.

Along this road I travel
to wherever I'm going,
all is sad and pitiful.
. . . .
I think right here where I am
where I'm thinking,
that one day we will have JOY!)

The poem treats black suffering within an archetypal/mythical/biblical frame through metaphors associated with the scapegoat and the perpetual Other. Dedicated to "Nicolás Guillén and all the people of his race," this poem brings into clear focus an issue that is very prevalent in Venezuela today. The Ham metaphor, which appeared earlier in Rodríguez Cárdenas and Díaz Sánchez, remains a burden for Afro-Venezuelans. The difference between the three authors is that Antonio Acosta Márquez is not prepared to accept perpetual suffering.

The fact that sentiments in Acosta Márquez's works regarding the black experience have not been expressed in print until now certainly does not mean they haven't been felt by others. The poet makes it clear to the reader that he's aware of his culture but, at the same time, it will require more than cultural affirmation to throw off the yokes of Venezuelan classism and racism.

The first edition of *I Think Right Here Where . . . I Am* is a cry for recognition of and respect for Afro-Venezuelans. The poet views the entire black population of Barlovento as exploited, rootless people who have been forced away from the essential values that have sustained them for centuries. As they move closer toward the miscegenated national center, this trend is likely to continue. The poet appeals to their collective memory not to forget.

In the revised edition of *I Think Right Here Where . . . I Am* (1981), Antonio Acosta Márquez continues to write within the mythic constructs of Afro-Venezuelan culture. The author insists more upon the Afro dimension of their shared, learned behavior as being essential in their struggle for liberation. There are fourteen new poems in the section "Canto al son de mi ancestro" ("Canto to the Song of My Ancestry"), several of which are devoted to liberation through either education or armed resistance. "Yumba Maku," "Canto para despertar un negrito" ("Song to Awaken a Little Black Boy"), and "Son Afrolatino" ("Afro-Latin Song") are representative of this trend.

"Yumba Maku" is an invocation to battle that commences with a slave chant, a call for revolution in the defiant maroon tradition. The poem begins with a choral introito:

E-E-E-E. YUMBA
YUMBA, MAKU, CANTO.
E-E-E-E-. YUMBA
QUE SE CALIENTE LO CUERO
QUE SE CALIENTE EL TAMBOL.
QUE SE CALIENTE LO NEGRO
Y BUQUEN LIBERACION (bis)[7]

7. *Yo pienso aquí donde . . . Estoy,* 2d ed. (Caracas: Editorial Trazos, 1981), 34. This book has been expanded and divided into four sections: "Canto al son de mis ancestros" ("Song to the Music of My Ancestors"), "Canto en tono mayor" ("Song in a Major Chord"), "Canto de causa y costumbre" ("Song of Purpose and Custom"), and

. . . .
(LET'S HEAT UP THE LEATHER
LET'S HEAT UP THE DRUM.
LET'S HEAT UP THE BLACK
AND SEARCH FOR LIBERATION) (Repeat)

The rhythmic tone of the poem is established through the initial cry and alliteration and anaphora constructed around the vibrant image of *caliente* (heat), which suggests positive action. The poem's discourse is in the form of popular speech, a dialogue between two Barloventeños regarding the historical role of blacks under oppression and their search for liberation.

"Yumba Maku" is framed within a series of rhetorical questions relevant to the Afro-Venezuelan's relation to the national context. The motivating force behind the poem is the son of Asunción, who has taken up arms and joined the guerrilla movement. The technique used to develop the poem is a dichotomy between an informed and an uninformed speaker; these two speakers assess the current situation of blacks. They are divided between accepting the status quo and calling upon a long history of struggle to place the present in its proper perspective.

¿Quién abito negro tumbando . . .
tumbando Gobielno . . . ?
Si el negro nació . . . si el negro nació
pa, siempre sé esclabo,
y pa, calga saco,
y pa, lleba cuero . . .
¿Quién abito negro,
siendo guerrillero?
Negro pal trabajo,
negro pa, sé obrero.
¿Quién abito negro?
¿Quién abito negro . . .
tumbando Gobielno?

(34)

(Who has seen a black overthrowing . . .
overthrowing the Government . . . ?
If the black was born . . . if the black was born
they were always to be enslaved,
and, to carry sacks,

"Recuerdo triste de mi infancia obrera" ("Sad Remembrance of My Working-Class Childhood"). All further references in this chapter are to the second edition.

and, to carry hides . . .
Who has seen a black
being a guerrilla?
The black is for working
the black is a worker.
Who has seen a black?
Who has seen a black . . .
overthrowing the Government?)

"Who has seen a black" reinforces a series of incredulous parallels
in which the capacity of the black to function as a maker of history is
questioned. Ironically, the role of Afro-Venezuelans as victims is
highlighted by a naive witness without regard for the long par-
ticipation of blacks in maroonage, in the Independence Wars from
Spain, and in the armies of the numerous *caudillos* who have marched
through Venezuelan history. The role of the Afro-Venezuelan as
slave, laborer, and exploited being has replaced most of that glo-
rious past, at least in the mind of one of the speakers. Irony and the
rhetorical question, as poetic devices, capture skillfully this frank
exchange.

One of the poem's interlocutors also does not seem to comprehend why Asunción's son, who is educated, would wish to join the
guerrilla movement. The answer to that dilemma, too, is implied
through a rhetorical question:

—¿Qué tenemo nojotro,
que no seajeno . . . ?
No quitan la playa.
No quitan terreno
Jata se lleban
nuestra tradición.

(35)

(—What do we have
that is not foreign . . . ?
They've taken away the beach.
They've taken away land
They've even carried away
our tradition.)

Those with education are more likely to see the effects of exploitation from different perspectives than those limited to their immediate circumstances. Bereft of ancestral culture and acquired material
goods and overwhelmed by outside influences, the most important
goals worth fighting for are respect, dignity, and self-determination:

Si yo tubiera joven
me alzaría también
me juera pal monte
a la rebolución
polque la juelza ta siempre
onde ai unión.
y miría cantado
aquella canción . . .
que cantaban lo eclabo
alzao aquí en mi región.
                                        (36)

(If I were young
I would rise up too
I would go to the mountain
to the revolution
because force is always
where there's union.
and I would be singing
that song . . .
which the rebellious slaves
of my region sang.)

The informed voice offers unmitigated support for the implementa-
tion of historically based resistance to the oppressive conditions
existing in Barlovento. Throughout their history force has been an
instrument for change and the same holds true if they are to prosper
in modern society. Based upon past experiences, the people of Barlovento will have to assume responsibility for their own destiny
through action.

Education, as a motivating force for change, is also the primary
motif of "Song to Awaken a Black Child." There have been several
well-known songs to put children to sleep, but this poem presents
an ironic difference. It too begins with the chorus:

CALAMEE, CALAMEE, CALAMEE
CUN-CUN-CALEE-MAA.
AY . . . CALAMEE, CALAMEE, CALAMEE
CALAMEE, CUN-CUN, CALEE-MAA (bis)
                                        (42)

It is a collective reminder to black youth of their responsibility:

Estudia negro pa, Benezuela.
Estudia negro pa, Balobento.

A vé si así sacamo al patrón
que no tiene tolció el cuello.
Mijo no estudie pacete rico.
Quiero que aprenda mijo pal pueblo.
Pa, quenseñe aquel que no sabe
Pa, quenseñe a tuelmano negro.
(42–43)

(Study blacks for, Venezuela.
Study blacks for, Barlovento.
Let's see if that way we get rid of the boss
who has us by the throat.
My son don't study to be rich.
I want you to learn for the people.
So you will teach what it doesn't know
So you will teach all your black brothers.)

Ignorance on the part of blacks reinforces the level of exploitation meted out by the oppressor. Education will at least assure a different way of viewing the world and allow the socially committed individual to question some of the prevalent social practices that work to the disadvantage of an entire ethnic group.

Of these three selections treating cultural maroonage, "Son Afrolatino" ("Afrolatin Song") serves as an affirmation of black values and calls for solidarity within the more insular cultural context of Barlovento:

Si digo Afrolatino
tino . . . tino tengo yo,
Afro que biene de Africa,
Ca . . . ca . . . ramba
QUE BUENO SUENA MI SON.
(44)

(If I say Afrolatin
wisdom . . . I have wisdom
Afro which comes from Africa
My word
HOW GOOD MY SONG SOUNDS.)

This wisdom that the poet possesses will be used to protect the cultural integrity of his region. The drum, the dances, and the work songs all reinforce the region's cultural unity. The poet warns against intruders:

Ese musiú e malo
bailando tambol
Ese gringo e malo
peroai otro pió,
mirale lo diente,
aguaitale la pata,
con bota americana
tambol no se baila
(45)

(That foreigner is evil
dancing to the drum
That gringo is evil
but there's another who's worse,
look at his teeth,
check out his feet,
with American boots
you don't dance to the drum)

This hermetic attitude is understandable, considering the manner in which Afro-Venezuelan culture has been interpreted, studied, and transmitted by outsiders who have not always had the best interests of its producers at heart. Therefore, the burden is upon Afro-Venezuelans to maintain and reaffirm what is historically theirs and what is essential to their existence.

Indeed, one of the major achievements of *I Think Right Here Where . . . I Am* is to keep the literary dimension of Afro-Venezuelan popular culture alive and vital. Poems devoted to the drum culture, culinary tradition, the spiritualist tradition, and superstition underscore the importance of tradition within the definition and distillation of life in Barlovento.

The poet also demonstrates an awareness of those who do not act in the best interests of unity. "Gua . . . Gua . . . Qué Cara" ("My . . . My . . . What a Face") is a negative portrayal of the police, who cannot change their repressive tactics no matter their rank. "El Negro 'Pedro los Ruedo' " ("Black Pedro Ruedo") is an ironic presentation of a *negro* who threatens his own kind because of the sense of power he draws from association with the ruling structures. "La Loca María Poleo" ("Crazy María") recounts the antics of a madwoman who goes about insulting blacks and pretending that she is white and important. These poems demonstrate that, as in many communities, there are many different forces in contention in Venezuela that have varying impacts upon the population. Divisiveness of the sort portrayed here can lead only to further deterioration of black identity.

In this revised section of the volume, the poet continues to demonstrate his concern for future generations. "El Negrito Mandinga" ("Black Mandinga") is about a devilish black child who is motivated by fun and games more than serious endeavors. The message is, work hard and learn, since the opportunities are available. On the other hand, "Pelito Pegón" ("Little Poor One") addresses the issues of poverty, homelessness, and the abandonment of the street urchins of Barlovento. Their plight is captured in these moving verses:

Beo en tu semblante
elambre malcá
de niño sin padre
y madre abandoná
pelito pegón
pelito quemao,
zapatico roto
Piecito ampollao.
(37)

(I see hunger marked
in your face
of a fatherless child
and abandoned mother
Penniless one
Burned out,
worn out shoes
little blistered feet.)

Despite the desperate plight of this urchin, the poet, who is forever optimistic, looks to the future for redemption as he again evokes the awakening metaphor: "depeltará pronto, / berá nueba aurora / cambiará tu bida / negro totao" (you will awaken soon / you will see a new dawn / your life will change / sunburnt black). Perhaps with a strong sense of identity and a firm grounding in Afro-Venezuelan culture, future generations will be prepared for the many obstacles they must overcome.

Antonio Acosta Márquez's poetry is a rare, positive, contemporary interpretation of the Afro-Venezuelan experience. The poet not only identifies with blackness but also possesses a knowledge of culture and the ability to articulate it in verse in a clear and meaningful fashion. As the bard of Barlovento, Acosta Márquez is in tune with the private lives of the people and the *intrahistoria* of the region, and he has some understanding regarding what the people's needs are. It is precisely this *identification* with Afro-Venezuelans that separates Acosta Márquez from Rodríguez Cárdenas as a poet of the black experience. Acosta Márquez neither calls for "bettering the race" through miscegenation nor does he denigrate or dehumanize his black protagonists. Rather, Acosta Márquez deals with blacks on their own terms while implicitly questioning and resisting the process of deafricanization.

CONCLUSION

If Not Now, When?

The debate regarding ethnicity, color, class, and racism in Venezuela has not subsided. Professor Ligia J. Montañéz recently presented to the School of Psychology at the Universidad Central de Venezuela a "trabajo de ascenso" (thesis for promotion) entitled "Prejuicios étnicos hacia los negros en Venezuela: El rasgo oculto de una sociedad no racista" ("Ethnic Prejudices Toward Blacks in Venezuela: The Hidden Trait of a Nonracist Society"). This work, which has yet to be published, received an honorable mention in the 1990 Casa de las Américas competition. During a radio forum that aired on March 5, 1990, Professor Montañéz defended her ideas regarding the current situation of blacks in Venezuela.

Professor Montañéz's premise concerning discrimination against Afro-Venezuelans was expressed in an earlier article and expanded in her recent work. Under the heading "Somos una sociedad racista" ("We Are a Racist Society") she concludes: "I would like to return to the questions that I raised at the beginning. The theme treated is racism, we do not find another word. It is not pseudoracism or quasiracism. No. It has to do with racist components, different from our racism of yesterday, but children of it. As a result it is a bit violent to say it and, of course, even more to accept it."[1] Before arriving at this conclusion, the author delineates the impact of racism and discrimination upon many aspects of Afro-Venezuelan life, economic, social, and family life in particular. The resulting pressure forces blacks to try and abandon the *Afro* of their heritage, seeking refuge in miscegenation, a process which has been ongoing since their arrival in Venezuela.

Needless to say, Professor Montañéz's research is at odds with the official ideology regarding interethnic dynamics in Venezuela. According to this ideology, Venezuelans are Venezuelans and, regard-

1. "La discriminación racial," 449.

107

less of color, one homogeneous nation—"café con leche" (coffee with cream). Afro-Venezuelans have no choice, even if they want one, but to accept national doctrines concerning race and class, because the majority internalizes and practices the tendency toward miscegenation, that is, the desire to "mejorar la raza" (improve the race) by eliminating the black component.

In October 1990, Venezuela conducted its official census, utilizing a questionnaire that covered six broad areas: (1) Localización geográfica. Datos de la vivienda (Geographical location. Housing statistics); (2) Características de la población (Characteristics of the population); (3) Características generales (General characteristics); (4) Características educativas (Educational characteristics); (5) Características de fecundidad (Birth rate characteristics); and (6) Características económicas (Economic characteristics).[2] The issue of ethnicity is not raised within any of these categories, a practice that will assure a harmonious accounting for all of those Venezuelans who respond.

The point to be made here is that there is a discrepancy between official and real perceptions of color in Venezuelan society, a situation that is not likely to change. The fact that creative writers make these incongruities central to their literary creations is not surprising. In each of the four writers studied here, there is a degree of ambivalence toward issues of ethnicity, which they present based upon experience, ideology, and perceptions.

Juan Pablo Sojo was successful in his time because he was perceived as "folkloric" and, in addition, opened up the Afro-Venezuelan world to investigators such as Juan Liscano, Pedro Lhaya, and others. Manuel Rodríguez Cárdenas grew up in a black Venezuelan environment, recognized the *negrista* trends in Spanish America, participated in them, and was rebuffed for his activities. For Ramón Díaz Sánchez, the Afro-Venezuelan experience was purely an intellectual, literary exercise with the underlying purpose of demonstrating white superiority. Antonio Acosta Márquez, though relatively unknown and ignored, emerged as a virile voice, refocusing attention on the plight of blacks in Venezuela and demonstrating that they are not culturally extinct. As a talented, sensitive, and sophisticated writer, Acosta Márquez's works deserve the same critical scrutiny as that received by his Venezuelan counterparts. It is unlikely this will happen.

Drum and *Cumboto* were written by *pardo/mulato/mestizo* writers who were fascinated by black culture. These works are technically

2. Hugo Colmenares, "Empadronamiento nacional será el 28 de octubre," C4.

of good artistic quality. Their main fault is that the authors do not transcend a surface understanding of the people they attempt to portray, and they therefore lack the important element of authenticity. Within this context, both authors display insensitivity toward black culture in their presentations of black characters and circumstances.

Black St. John's Eve and *I Think Right Here Where . . . I Am* are perceived as folklore in Venezuela, and subsequently they have not been the serious objects of study of literary critics. The works are designed to create and sustain an Afro-Venezuelan discourse, having an underlying conceptual basis that accentuates the mythic dimension of Barlovento. The mythic structure of these two works, which is collective and communal and buttresses the culturalist approach employed here, encompasses folklore, drum culture, language, the maroon experience, and the struggle for liberation. Through literature, the authors fuse learned aspects of the African experience with lived Venezuelan reality from the perspective of the oppressed. Sojo and Acosta Márquez are yet to be viewed as serious creative writers in Veneuzuela.

In the introduction to her brief study and anthology of Venezuelan poetry, *El devenir de la palabra poética: Venezuela siglo XX* (*The Emergence of the Poetic Word: Venezuela the Twentieth Century*), Vilma Vargas takes a rather self-righteous attitude toward the development of that genre:

> We believe that we lack poets as influential as some of the chosen ones, but nevertheless the selection serves as an indication of the poetic lines that have been drawn in the country. We have cast aside that popular troubadorish trend that has proliferated so much, above all in an era, by considering that in the majority of cases, its authors are verse writers more than poets. We have also cast aside that "poetry" which has been converted by the author, more than into a necessity, into a medium. A medium which will help obtain publicity, social success, etc.[3]

For Vilma Vargas, writing a decade ago, Venezuelan poetry is that which seeks to imitate the masters of the Western tradition by incorporating their imagery, style, form, and content. The further away from a Venezuelan frame of reference a poet can get, the better.

The popular and learned trends in Venezuelan poetry are still at odds, as is exemplified by two recent events. From February 19 to 22, 1990, Professor Armando Rojas Guardia presented a series of four lectures entitled "La poesía Venezolana desde los 60 hasta los 80"

---

3. *El devenir de la palabra poética: Venezuela siglo XX,* 21.

("Venezuelan Poetry from the '60s to the '80s") at the Sala Mendoza
in Caracas. His focus was "universalismo" and "modernización" as
he proceeded to situate the poetic movements and authors in Venezuela within trends such as "surrealismo" and "cosmopolitanismo"
from Juan Sánchez Peláez to the present. About a dozen subscribers
were in attendance; I was present at two of the lectures.

Interestingly enough, the week before, on February 16, 1990,
there had been a rally in the Plaza Caracas to commemorate the fifth
anniversary of the death of Alí Primera, perhaps the most renowned
contemporary poet in Venezuela. Hundreds of people attended the
rally, including myself. Commenting upon the far-reaching impact
of this poet, José Vicente Rangel remembers that "his poetry was, in
essence, a product of what he gathered from the poor people. Words,
verses, anecdotes, experiences, derived from the purest of popular
feelings. His protest never was a headline or an enterprising product of political meditations. He was a clearly defined and committed
man, but one who made concessions neither to elitism nor to dog-
ma."[4] It goes without saying that the poetry of Alí Primera will
probably not be consecrated in the halls of institutions of higher
learning in Venezuela. Neither will the works of Antonio Acosta
Márquez. Alí Primera wrote in the introduction to *I Think Right Here
Where. . . I Am:* "Nothing is as beautiful as simplicity, and that is the
vital essence of this popular poet. That class of poet who does not
lose his memory." Acosta Márquez certainly has not lost the ethnic
memory of his beloved Barlovento. It is too bad that the critical
establishment in Venezuela remembers to forget his work and that
of other Afro-Venezuelans.[5]

---

4. "Alí Primera," A6.
5. The only Venezuelan reactions to Antonio Acosta Márquez's poetry I have been
able to locate are the brief remarks contained in "El barrio, el caribe y Barlovento
hace sonar la otra cultura," 24.

BIBLIOGRAPHY

Articles

Agudo Freites, Raúl. "Cincuenta años de *Nochebuena negra.*" *Revista nacional de cultura* 39.238 (1978): 23–32.

Alvarez D'Armas, Arturo. "Bibliografía afrovenezolana." *Ultimas noticias: Suplemento cultural* (16 January 1977): 8.

———. "El negro en la obra de Juan Pablo Sojo." *Ultimas noticias: Suplemento cultural* (24 October 1976): 8.

Aray, Edmundo. "La actual literatura de Venezuela." In *Panorama de la actual literatura latinoamericana,* 113–36. Caracas: Editorial Fundamentos, 1971.

Ayala, Delia. "En torno a *Cumboto:* Supersticiones de un mundo primitivo y ardiente." *El universal: Indice literario* (29 June 1965): 1.

"El barrio, el caribe y Barlovento hace sonar la otra cultura." *El diario de Caracas: Sección cultural* (24 October 1979): 24.

Beane, Carol. "Mestizaje: 'Civilización' or 'Barbarie'—Prospects for Cultural Continuity in *Matalaché, Pobre Negro,* and *Cumboto.*" *Studies in Afro-Hispanic Literature* 2–3 (1978–1979): 199–212.

Belrose, Maurice. "L'Afrique au colur de Venezuela." *Notre librairie* 80 (1985): 76–84.

Colmenares, Hugo. "Empadronamiento nacional será el 28 de octubre." *El Nacional* (28 February 1990): C4.

Cuadernos Afro-Americanos 1.1 (1975).

Cyrus, Stanley. "Ethnic Ambivalence and Afro-Hispanic Novelists." *Afro-Hispanic Review* 1.1 (1982): 29–32.

De Caracas, Juan. "Excursión hacia el negro venezolano." *Elite* 17.836 (11 October 1941): 17–19, cont. 65–66.

Díaz Sánchez, Ramón. "La brujería." *Elite* 10.478 (6 October 1934): 18–19, cont. 72–74.

———. "El mulato." *El Heraldo: Página literaria* (3 July 1938): 15.

———. "Negros y blancos." *El Universal* (12 June 1950): 4.

———. "Perspectivas históricas de la cultura venezolana: Lo Español y lo Africano." *Revista nacional de cultura* 24.223 (1963): 35–51.

"Ensayo: Averiguación del mulato en *Tambor.*" *El Heraldo: Página literaria* (3 July 1938): 15.

Flores, Angel. "Magical Realism in Spanish American Fiction." *Hispania* 38.2 (1955): 187–92.

García Hernández, Manuel. "La novela *Cumboto* y el racismo." *El universal: Artes y letras* (14 May 1950): 2.

Geisdorfer Feal, Rosemary. "Patriarchism and Racism: The Case of *Cumboto*." *Afro-Hispanic Review* 2.1 (1983): 25–28.

Hampton, Janet J. "Music and Dance as Media of Character Analysis and Affirmation of a Black Aesthetic in *Cumboto*." *Afro-Hispanic Review* 10.1 (1991): 3–9.

Kubayanda, Josaphat B. "Afrocentric Hermeneutics and the Rhetoric of 'Transculturación' in Black Latin American Literature." In *Proceedings of the October 1983 Conference of the Canadian Association for Latin American and Caribbean Studies,* edited by Arch R. M. Ritter, 226–40. Ottawa, Canada: Carleton University School of International Affairs, 1984.

———. "Minority Discourse and the African Collective: Some Examples from Latin American and Caribbean Literature." *Cultural Critique* 6 (1987): 113–30.

———. "Notes on the Impact of African Oral-Tradition Rhetoric on Latin American and Caribbean Writing." *Afro-Hispanic Review* 3.3 (1984): 5–10.

Leal, Luis. "El realismo mágico en la literatura hispanoamericana." *Cuadernos Americanos* 4 (July-August 1967): 230–35.

Lhaya, Pedro. "El tema negro en la literatura venezolana." *Imagen* 110 (1977): 34–38.

Liscano, Juan. "Apuntes para la investigación del negro en Venezuela: Sus instrumentos de música." *Acta venezolana* 1.4 (1946): 421–40.

———. "Las fiestas del solsticio de verano en el folklore de Venezuela." *Revista nacional de cultura* 63 (1947): 31–51.

Megenney, William W. "Africa en Venezuela: Su herencia lingüística y su cultura literaria." *Montalbán* 15 (1984): 207–60.

———. "Black Rural Speech in Venezuela." *Afro-Hispanic Review* 7.1–3 (1988): 39–44.

———. "Themes of Socio-Ethnic Awareness in the Oral Literature of Venezuelan Blacks." *Afro-Hispanic Review* 8.1–2 (1989): 3–8.

Meneses, Guillermo. "*Nochebuena negra:* Novela de Barlovento." *Ahora* (25 July 1943): 12–13.

———. "Veinticinco años de novela venezolana." *Revista nacional de cultura* 161 (1963): 207–24.

Montañéz, Ligia. "La discriminación racial." *SIC* 50.500 (1987): 445–49.

Mullen, Edward. "The Emergence of Afro-Hispanic Poetry: Some Notes on Canon Formation." *Hispanic Review* 56 (1988):435–53.

"Nuestra africanidad." *El Nacional: Papel literario.* Caracas (6 November 1977): 1–4. Four interviews with Margarita D'Amico:

1. Miguel Acosta Saignes, "La herencia africana," 1.

2. Federico Brito Figueroa, "La población negra en la historia económica y social de Venezuela," 2.

3. Juan Liscano, "El aporte negro en las artes y la transculturación," 3.

4. José Marcial Ramos Guédez, "Testimonio de las nuevas generaciones," 4.

Olivares Figueroa, Rafael. "*Cumboto:* Novela de negros y mulatos." *El Universal: Indice literaria* (24 January 1961): 1.

Ortiz, Alexis. "Sucesos y personajes" (Antonio Acosta Márquez). *Revista intimidades* (7 September 1978): no page number.

Persico, Alan. "Ramón Díaz Sánchez: Primitive or Creator?" *Afro-Hispanic Review* 5.1–3 (1986): 13–17.

———. "*La virgen no tiene cara:* A Portrayal of Rebellion in Afro-Hispanic Narrative." *Afro-Hispanic Review* 3.3 (1984): 11–15.

Pollak-Eltz, Angelina. "Household Composition and Mating Patterns Among Lower-Class Venezuelans." In *Urbanization in the Americas from the Beginnings to the Present,* edited by Richard P. Schadel, Jorge Enrique Hardoy, and Nora Scott Kinzer, 526–36. Paris: Mouton, 1978.

———. "Socialization of Children Among Afro-Venezuelans." *International Social Science Journal* 31.3 (1979): 470–76.

"Racismo nuestro." *SIC* 45.442 (1982): 52–67.

1. María Eugenia Villalón, "Discriminación vs. indianidad," 52–55.

2. Ignacio Castillo S., "El umbral de color," 56–60.

3. Pedro Trigo, "Patria, la mestiza," 61–64.

4. José Marcial Ramos Guédez, "Los descendientes de Africanos," 65.

5. Otto Maduro, "Clases y razas," 66–67.

Ramos Guédez, José Marcial. "El trabajo de los esclavos negros en el valle de Caracas y zonas ayacentes en el siglo XVIII." In *Primer congreso de la cultura negra de las Américas,* edited by Manuel Zapata Olivella, 121–43. Bogotá: Fundación Colombiana de Investigaciones Folklóricas, 1988.

Rangel, José Vicente. "Alí Primera." *El Nacional* (22 February 1990): A6.

Richards, Henry. "A Look at the Narrative Structure of *Cumboto.*" *Studies in Afro-Hispanic Literature* 2–3 (1978–1979): 134–51.

Rogmann, Horst. "Realismo mágico y 'negritude' como construcciones ideológicas." *Ideologies and Literatures* 2.10 (1979): 45–55.

Rojas Jiménez, Oscar. "Geografía lírica de la región negra venezolana." *Revista nacional de cultura* 2 (1938): 5–8.

Smart, Ian I. "The Afro-Hispanic Review." In *Philosophy and Literature in Latin America: A Critical Assessment of the Current Situation,* edited by Jorge García and Mireya Camurati, 194–200. Albany: State University of New York Press, 1988.

———. "The Trickster Pícaro in Three Contemporary Afro-Hispanic Novels." *Afro-Hispanic Review* 7.1–3 (1988): 49–52.

Smyley, Karen. "The Sensate Universe in *Cumboto* and *Batouala*." *Afro-Hispanic Review* 2.2 (1983): 17–21.

Sojo, Juan Pablo. "Algunas supervivencias negro-culturales en Venezuela." In *El Estado Miranda: Sus tierras y sus hombres,* edited by Agusto Márquez Canisales, 269–82. Caracas: Editorial Sucre, 1959.

———. "Allá en las cumbres." In *El Estado Miranda: Sus tierras y sus hombres,* edited by Agusto Márquez Canisales, 217–33.Caracas: Editorial Sucre, 1959.

———. "La canción del tambor." *El Nacional* (20 October 1948): 9.

———. "Cofradías etno-africanas en Venezuela." *Cultura universitaria* 1 (1947): 97–103.

———. "El color del amor: Una comedia de Juan Pablo Sojo." *El Nacional* (27 April 1946): 11.

———. "Material para un glosario de afro-negrismos de Venezuela." In *Juan Pablo Sojo: Estudios del folklore venezolano,* edited by Juan Pablo Sojo Cardozo, 317–32. Los Teques, Venezuela: Biblioteca de Autores y Temas Mirandinos, 1986.

———. "Notas para un estudio sobre el regimen esclavista en Venezuela." In *Juan Pablo Sojo: Estudios del folklore venezolano,* edited by Juan Pablo Sojo Cardozo, 264. Los Teques, Venezuela: Biblioteca de Autores y Temas Mirandinos, 1986.

———. "Negro, tú caminas." *El Nacional* (20 October 1948): 9.

———. "Sambarambule." *El Nacional* (20 October 1948): 8.

———. "La tradición negra en el cuento y la leyenda." *El Nacional* (9 November 1947): 9.

———. "Zambo." *Ahora* (13 June 1943): 12.

Sommers, Joseph. "From the Critical Premise to the Product: Critical Modes and Their Applications to a Chicano Literary Text." *New Scholar* 6 (1977): 51–62.

Wright, Winthrop R. "Elitist Attitudes toward Race in Twentieth-Century Venezuela." In *Slavery and Race Relations in Latin America,* edited by Robert Brent Toplin, 325–47. Westport, Conn.: Greenwood Press, 1974.

Books and Dissertations

Acosta Márquez, Antonio. *Yo pienso aquí donde . . . Estoy.* Medellin: Editorial Cascabel, 1977. 2d ed. Caracas: Editorial Trazos, 1981.

Acosta Saignes, Miguel. *Vida de los esclavos negros en Venezuela*. Caracas: Hespérides Ediciones, 1967.

Anderson Imbert, Enrique. *El realismo mágico y otros ensayos*. Caracas: Monte Avila, 1976.

Angulo, María Elena. "Realismo maravilloso and Social Context in Five Modern Latin American Novels". Ph.D. diss., University of California-Berkeley, 1989.

Aranda, Sergio. *Las clases sociales y el estado en Venezuela*. Caracas: Editorial Pomaire, 1983.

Aretz, Isabel. *Manual de folklore*. Caracas: Monte Avila, 1984.

————. *El Tamunangue*. Barquisimeto, Estado Lara: Ediciones de la Universidad Centro-Occidental, 1970.

Arujo, Orlando. *Narrativa venezolana contemporánea*. Caracas: Tiempo Nuevo, 1972.

Asante, Molefi Kete. *The Afrocentric Idea*. Philadelphia: Temple University Press, 1987.

Bansart, Andres. *El negro en la litertura hispanoamericana: Bibliografía y hemerografía*. Caracas: Editorial de la Universidad Simón Bolivar, 1986.

Belrose, Maurice. *Presence du noir dans le roman venezuelien*. Antilles-Guyane: Editions Caribeennes, 1981.

————. *La sociedad venezolana en su novela, 1890–1935*. Maracaibo-Universidad del Zulia: Facultad de Humanidades y Educación Centro de Estudios Literarios, 1979.

Brandt, Max Hans. "An Ethnomusicological Study of Three Afro-Venezuelan Drum Ensembles of Barlovento." Doctoral thesis, Queens University, Belfast, Northern Ireland, 1978.

Brookshaw, Michael Anthony. "Protest, Militancy, and Revolution: The Evolution of the Afro-Hispanic Novel of the Diaspora." Ph.D. diss., University of Illinois-Urbana, 1983.

Brotherston, Gordon. *Latin American Poetry: Origin and Presence*. New York: Cambridge University Press, 1975.

Cardozo, Lubio and Juan Pinto. *Seudonimia literaria venezolana*. Mérida, Venezuela: Universidad de los Andes, 1974.

Carpentier, Alejo. *Tientos y diferencias*. 1967. Reprint. Buenos Aires: Calicanto Editorial, 1976.

Carrera, Gustavo Luis and Federico Vetencourt. *Los tambores de San Juan*. Caracas: Biblioteca de la Universidad Central, 1964.

Chacón, Alfredo. *Curiepe*. Caracas: Universidad Central de Venezuela, 1979.

————. *Poblaciones y culturas negras de Venezuela*. Caracas: Instituto Autónomo Biblioteca Nacional y de Servicios de Bibliotecas, 1983.

Davis, Robert C. and Ronald Schleifer. *Contemporary Literary and Cultural Studies*. 2d ed. New York: Longman, 1989.

Díaz Sánchez, Ramón. *Ambito y acento: Para una teoría de la venezola-nidad.* Caracas: Editorial Elite, 1938.

———. *Cam, ensayo sobre el negro.* Maracaibo: El País, 1933.

———. *Cumboto.* Caracas: Editorial Mediterráneo, 1950.

———. *Paisaje histórico de la cultura venezolana.* Buenos Aires: Editorial Universitaria, 1965.

Díaz Seijas, Pedro. *La antigua y la moderna literatura venezolana: Estudio histórico-crítico, con antología.* Caracas: Ediciones Armitaño, 1966.

Dixon, Sandra. "Racial Identity and Literary Image: The Characteriza-tion of Afro-Hispanics and Whites in Selected Novels of Venezu-ela and Brazil." Ph.D. diss., Brown University, 1986.

García, Jesús Chucho. *Contra el cepo: Barlovento tiempo de cimarrones.* Barlovento, Venezuela: Editorial Lucas y Trina, 1989.

Guerra Cedeño, Franklin. *Esclavos negros, cimarroneras y cumbres de Bar-lovento.* Caracas: Cuadernos Lagoven, 1984.

Irazabal, Carlos. *Venezuela, esclava y feudal.* Caracas: Editorial Ateneo de Caracas, 1980.

Jackson, Richard L. *The Afro Spanish-American Author II: The 1980s. An Annotated Bibliography of Recent Criticism.* West Cornwall, Conn: Locust Hill Press, 1989.

Jackson, Shirley M. *La novela negrista en hispanoamerica.* Madrid: Edi-torial Pliegos, 1986.

Lhaya, Pedro. *Juan Pablo Sojo: Pasión y acento de su tierra.* Caracas: In-stituto Nacional de Cultura y Bellas Artes, 1968.

Liscano, Juan. *La Fiesta de San Juan el Bautista.* Caracas: Monte Avila, 1973.

———. *Folklore y cultura: Ensayos.* Caracas: Editorial Avila Gráfica, 1950.

———, ed. *Poesía popular venezolana.* Caracas: Ediciones al Servicio de la Cultura, 1945.

Liscano, Juan, and Isabel Aretz. *El Mampulorio.* Caracas: Imprenta del Ministerio de Educación, 1956.

McKinley, Michael P. *Pre-Revolutionary Caracas: Politics, Economy, and Society, 1777–1811.* New York: Cambridge University Press, 1985.

Madriz Galindo, Fernando. *Una visión de Barlovento.* Los Teques: Casa de la Cultura, 1969.

Márquez Canisales, Agusto, ed. *El Estado Miranda: Sus tierras y sus hombres.* Caracas: Editorial Sucre, 1959.

Martín, Gustavo. *Magia y religión en la Venezuela contemporánea.* Caracas: Ediciones de la Universidad Central de Venezuela, 1983.

Mbiti, John S. *African Religions and Philosophy.* New York: Praeger Pub-lishers, 1969.

Novo Cabal, María Teresa. *La literatura popular afrovenezolana.* Caracas: Editorial de la Universidad Simón Bolivar, 1984.

Núñez, Benjamín. *Dictionary of Afro-Latin American Civilization.* Westport, Conn.: Greenwood Press, 1980.

Olivares Figueroa, Rafael. *Nuevos poetas venezolanos: Notas críticas.* Caracas: Editorial Elite, 1939.

Panorama de la actual literatura latinoamericana. Caracas: Editorial Fundamentos, 1971.

Persico, Alan. "Ethnic Vision and Narrative Style: A Psychostylistic Analysis of Selected Works of Ramón Díaz Sánchez." Ph.D. diss., University of Illinois, 1983.

Piquet, Daniel. *La cultura afrovenezolana en sus escritores contemporáneos.* Caracas: Monte Avila, 1982.

Ramos Guédez, José Marcial. *Bibliografía afrovenezolana.* Caracas: Instituto Autónomo Biblioteca Nacional y de Servicios de Bibliotecas, 1980.

———. *El negro en la novela venezolana.* Caracas: Universidad Central de Venezuela, 1980.

———. *El negro en Venezuela: Aporte bibliográfico.* 2d ed. Caracas: Instituto Autónomo Biblioteca Nacional y de Servicios de Bibliotecas, 1985.

Ramón y Rivera, Luis Felipe. *El folklore en la novela venezolana.* Caracas: Contexto Editores, 1982.

———. *La música afrovenezolana.* Caracas: Universidad Central de Venezuela, 1971.

———. *La música folklórica de Venezuela.* Caracas: Monte Avila, 1969.

———. *Poesía afrovenezolana.* Caracas: Instituto de Folklore, 1970.

Ritter, Arch R. M., ed. *Proceedings of the October 1983 Conference of the Canadian Association for Latin American and Caribbean Studies.* Ottawa, Canada: Carleton University School of International Affairs, 1984.

Rodríguez Cárdenas, Manuel. *Entonces el pueblo era pequeño.* Caracas: Contraloria de la República, 1972.

———. *Poesías.* 2d ed. San Felipe: Sociedad Bolivariana Larista, 1968.

———. *Tambor: Poemas para negros y mulatos.* Caracas: Editorial Elite, 1938. 2d ed. Caracas: Contraloria de la Republica, 1972.

Sambrano Urdaneta, Oscar. *Apuntes críticos sobre "Cumboto."* Boconó, Venezuela: Editorial Cordillera, 1952.

———. *Contribución a una bibliografía general de la poesia venezolana en el siglo XX.* Caracas: Universidad Central de Venezuela, 1979.

Schwartz, Kessel. *A New History of Spanish-American Fiction.* Coral Gables: University of Miami Press, 1972.

Sequera de Seginini, Isbelia. *Estudio geo-económico de la región de Barlovento.* Caracas: Gobernación del Estado Miranda, 1976.

Sojo, Juan Pablo. *Nochebuena negra.* Caracas: Editorial Elite, 1943. 2d ed. Caracas: Monte Avila, 1972.

————. *Temas y apuntes afro-venezolanos*. Caracas: Tipografía La Nación, 1943.

Sojo Cardozo, Juan Pablo, ed. *Juan Pablo Sojo: Estudios del folklore venezolano*. Los Teques, Venezuela: Biblioteca de Autores y Temas Mirandinos, 1986.

Stephens, Thomas M. *Dictionary of Latin American Racial and Ethnic Terminology*. Gainesville: University of Florida Press, 1989.

Subero, Efraín. *Contribución a la bibliografía de Ramón Díaz Sánchez*. Caracas: Universidad Católica Andrés Bello, 1970.

Tejera, María Josefina. *Diccionario de venezolanismos, Tomo 1, A–I*. Caracas: Universidad Central de venezuela, 1983.

Toplin, Robert Brent, ed. *Slavery and Race Relations in Latin America*. Westport, Conn.: Greenwood Press, 1974.

Vargas, Vilma. *El devenir de la palabra poética: Venezuela siglo XX*. Caracas: Universidad Central de Venezuela, 1980.

Wright, Winthrop R. *Café con leche: Race, Class, and National Image in Venezuela*. Austin: University of Texas Press, 1990.

Zapata Olivella, Manuel. *Las claves mágicas de América: Raza, clase y cultura*. Bogotá: Plaza y Janés, 1989.

Zavala, Silvio, ed. *El mestizaje en la historia de Ibero-América*. México: Editorial Cultura, 1962.

INDEX

119